VAGUS NERVE

Feel Relaxed Within 10 Minutes and Fix Your Brain-Gut Axis in Psychiatric and Inflammatory Disorders

Matthew Brady

Summary

Introduction

The vagus nerve acts as the superhighway of the body, transporting input between the brain and the internal organs, and regulating the reaction of the body at rest and recovery periods. The broad nerve emerges from the brain and branches out to the neck and chest in various directions, where it is responsible for acts such as bringing sensory input from the skin of the ear, regulating the muscles you use to chew and speak, and affecting the immune system.

According to the Encyclopedia Britannica, the vagus is the 10th of 12 cranial nerves and stretches directly from the brain. Although we refer to the vagus nerve as singular, it is simply a pair of nerves that originate from the left and right side of the brain stem's portion of the medulla oblongata. According to Merriam-Webster, which is fitting, the nerve takes its name from the Latin term for roaming, since the vagus nerve is the largest and most commonly branching cranial nerve.

The vagus nerve provides the primary influence for the parasympathetic division of the nervous system, by roaming and spreading across the body: the rest-and-digest counterpoint to the fight-or-flight reaction of the sympathetic nervous system. The vagus nerve sends signals that slow heart and respiration levels and improve digestion when the body is not under threat. Control moves to the sympathetic system in times of stress which produces the opposite effect. The vagus nerve also brings feedback impulses back into the brain from internal organs, enabling the brain to keep track of the actions of the organs.

Vagus nerve stimulation has been useful in treating epileptic cases which do not respond to medication. Surgeons insert an electrode in the neck along the right branch of the vagus nerve, with a battery inserted beneath the collarbone. According to the Epilepsy Base, the electrode delivers daily nerve stimulation, which reduces or in extreme cases eliminates the abnormal brain activation that induces seizures. According to the Mayo Clinic, Europe accepted a vagus nerve stimulator that doesn't require surgical implantation.

Evidence has also shown that stimulation of the vagus nerve may be useful in the treatment of psychological disorders which do not respond to medication. Vagus nerve stimulation has been approved by the FDA for treatment-resistant depression and cluster headaches. A 2008 study published in the journal Brain Stimulation showed that stimulation of the vagus nerve contributed to an increase in symptoms for people with treatment-resistant anxiety disorders such as obsessive-compulsive disorder, panic disorder and post-traumatic stress disorder.

Most recently, researchers studied the function of the vagus nerve in treating chronic inflammatory diseases such as sepsis, lung disease, rheumatoid arthritis (RA) and diabetes, according to a study published in the Journal of Inflammation Research for 2018. Since the vagus nerve affects the immune system, nerve disruption may play a role in autoimmune diseases and other conditions.

Chapter 1: Nervous System

It collects both within and outside the body details—sensory feature. It Transmits information to the cortex and spinal retrieval regions. Processes brain and spinal information–convergence function. Sends input to muscle, gland, and organ so that they can respond to correctly-motor activity. It regulates and coordinates all vital functions of the body, and all other structures of the body that enable the body to retain homeostasis or its reactive equilibrium. Two main branches of the nervous system: the central nervous system (CNS) and the peripheral nervous system (PNS)

Basic cells of the nervous system Neurons

- Essential nervous system functional cells
- Carries impulses (up to 250 mph) parts of a neuron
- Dendrites-acquire stimulus and bring impulses into a cell body
- Body cells generating myelin or fat-layered cell
- Nucleus & most of cytoplasms
- Axons, fiber which takes impulses away from the cell body
- Schwann cells

- Excitability is the neuron to react and turn into a nervous impulse
- Most of Nothing Regulations
- The trigger is powerful enough to start, or nothing occurs
- Impulse also has equivalent energy in the neuron and is self-replication– as soon as it starts, the neuron moves in one direction only
- Synapse-a small distance or space between the axon of one neuron and another's dendrite-neurons don't necessarily stand up in synapse. This is the junction between neurons using neurotransmitters to activate the impulsion of the second neuron or effector (muscle, gland)

Reflex Arc:

- Receptor Materials–respond to stimulus
- Afferent pathway (sensory neuron) – spike to CNS
- Interneuron – consisting of one or two CNS synapses (most are spinal)
- Efferent pathway (engine neuron) refers to the effector of CNS impulses.
- Effector-Muscle fibers (as in the muscle Hamstring) or drums respond with the contraction and secretion of a drug.

Spinal reflexes-started and finished in the backbone. This occurs without the involvement of other brain centers.

1.1 Central Nervous System

Brain Spinal Cord

Meninges (Meninges are the three coverings around the brain & spinal cord, helping to cool, secure, and nourish the brain and spinal cord, which are the three coverings around the brain & spine.)

- Toughest outer layer
- Arachnoid mater is a middle layer which adheres to the dura mat which has poor attachments to the innermost layer, the pia mater
- Very thin translucent but durable pia mater is a very thin sheet, covering the whole brain, accompanied by the spines (sulcus) which spinal cord • cerebrospinal fluid that develops, supports, which detoxifies the brain. Cortex is the exterior portion (1.5 mm to 5 mm) between the cerebrum and cerebellum o. The Cortex is composed between folding bulges or gyri that produce deep furrows or gaps or sulci o. Folds in the brain are added to the surface area of the cerebral cortex, which enhances the volume of grey matter and the material that can be stored.
- Electrodes are mounted on the scalp using the EEG to test brain waves.

Four brainwaves are available:

- Beta
- Alpha
- Theta

- Delta

1.2 Peripheral Nervous System

• Relaying of the Somatic Nervous System (unconscious)

• Relaying information from the head, sensory organs and muscle-skeletal to the CNS

• Writing back to the skeletal muscles for voluntary Autonomic Nervous System responses (unconscious)

• Regulation of involuntary bodies

Key Sensation and Perception Organs

- Sight-Face
- Sound
- Smell-Olfactory system
- Body-hot, cold, heat, pain.

Eye - the organ responsible for detecting light

Three layers

• Sclera and cornea are the outer layer.

• The middle layer is made up of choroid, ciliary, and iris layer.

The inner layer consists of the retina structures of the major areas of the body: **sclera or scleroid layer**–a thick protective layer of connective tissue that helps preserve the body structure and matches the muscles pushing the eye cornea–a translucent dome-shaped portion of a sclera that protects the front of the eye, from which light reaches the eye Anterior C anterior portion. The neurological that transmits electrical impulses from the eye to the brain, like myopia or nearsightedness when the eyeball is too long or the cornea is too high, includes millions of photoreceptors (rods for black & white, and cones for colors) that turn light rays into electrical impulses that are transmitted through the brain by the optic nerve Optical nerve. Reorganized visual tract leaves the optical chiasm and travels to the lateral geniculate core

- Information is divided, ordered and connected to multiple visual cortex areas at the lateral geniculate core

- Perception and perception features are stored in separate areas of the visual cortex, obtained from both sensory and auditory fields.

EAR

External Ear & ear canal–carries sound to Eardrum–vibrates to enhance sound & divides inner and middle ear. The main ear has three small bones or osseicles= anvil, stirrup, sound amplification–sound amplification (little bones), which vibrates sound Eustachian tube, links the main of the ear with the mouth.

- The ear canal filters the sounds to the eardrum. A small, flexible membrane firmly wraps around the middle ear entrance.

- The waves are vibrating the eardrum.

• Such waves are passed to the hammer, one of three minuscule bones in the head. The vibrating hammer allows the anvil to vibrate, the thin bone that hits the hammer. The yellow passes these movements to the stirrup, another thin bone that contacts the black. The waves penetrate the inner ear from the stirrup.

• The stirrup touches a bag of liquid, and the waves penetrate a cochlea that is shaped like a cochlea.

• A vestibular network inside the cochlea made up of three semicircular tubes, which are in equal right angles to each other and responsible for a sense of balance and space orientation.

There are chambers filled with a viscous fluid and microscopic carbonate particles (otoliths). The displacement of this component of the inner ear over small hair cells gives signals to the brain that are perceived as motion and acceleration. The brain filters the input from the ear, which helps one to distinguish between specific sound forms.

Taste and Smell –Chemical Receptor Taste buds

• The mouth contains about 10,000 taste buds, most of which lie on and around tiny tongue bumps. Every taste bud senses five major tastes: o o Sour o Sweet o Bitter o Salty or Umami–other acid salts (e.g., monosodium glutamate or MSG)

• Each of the taste buds produces 50-100 specific receptor cells.

- Each of these receptor cells contains a tiny taste hair that tests for food chemicals in the saliva.
- Give nerve impulses to the brain while these taste hairs are activated.
- Every flavor hair better fits one of the five basic tastes. Smell receivers or olive receptors.
- Those who are able to sense thousands and thousands of various scents
- Olive receptors occupy a part of the nasal cavity wall, the empty room inside the nose
- Small fur, made of nerve fiber, originate from all the olfactory receptors. They are coated with a mucus coat.
- When a trace of chemicals dissolves in this mucus in the skin, the hair absorbs it and activates the olfactory receptors.
- A few molecules are necessary to activate these receptors, which are highly sensitive.
- Olfactory hair quickly sleepy, and you don't detect smells
- Linked to remembrances-when the olfactory receptors are activated, they send signals to your brain, and the pathway to the limbic system is immediately linked–a part of your mind that deals with impulses so that you can like or hate a scent.

Skin Receptors

Any of the touch receptors are on the surface of your skin.

Light-touching: Meissner's tissue corpuscles are wrapped in a contact envelope. They respond to a light-touch and are found in the skin of the hands, soils, lips, eyelashes, external genitals, and nipples.

High pressure

- Pacinian corpuscles profoundly affects the strength and sensation of the head.
- Each square centimeter of your skin has approximately 14 pressure receptor discomfort
- Transmitter
- Pain receptors are the numberest
- Each square centimeter of your skin has approximately 200 pain receivers temperature
- Skin transmitter hot and cold
- Per square centimeter of your skin includes six cold receivers and one hot receiver
- They are most excited when the skin surface is at 77 o F and when the skin surface decreases below 41 o F, they are no longer stimulated. That is why the feet or hands are numb for a long time when they are covered in beautiful mud.
- Hot reactors tend to experience hot feelings as the skin surface increases past 86 degrees F and is most excited

at 113 degrees F. In comparison to 113 o F, pain receptors are used to minimize injury to the skin and tissues.

- Thermosetters are located in the human body, but cold receptors are more concentrated than the heat receptor–generally cooler than the temperature of our corpses

- The greatest concentration of thermo setters is present on the face and ears so that the nose and ears get warmer even than the rest of the body on a cool day in the winter.

1.3 Disorders of the nervous system

Nervous system conditions-symptoms, diagnosis, treatment

- Epilepsy-specific and complex types of persistent epilepsy neurological disorders.

- Seizures-physical symptoms or behavioral changes that arise during an event in the brain with abnormal electrical activity induced by irregular electrical discharges into the brain

- Alzheimer's Disease- a degenerative brain disorder that causes dementia, a progressive deterioration with memory, cognition, and capacity to function.

- Compounded Sclerosis-autoimmune disease affecting the brain and spinal cord (central nervous system)-the body's immune system breaks off a defensive sheath of myelin that cover axons of the nerves and inhibits communication-MS can impair vision, feeling, balance, movements

- Parkinson's disease-neurological condition occurs in trembling and trouble walking balance, and coordination.

- Brain disorder: People with Parkinson's disease have reduced amounts of brain dopamine.

- Shingles-severe, blistering skin rashes from the chickenpox-causing varicella-zoster virus-stays dysfunctional in some nerves of the body (which is dormant).

Shingles arise after the virus is reactivated

- Cerebral paralysis

- Glaucoma – a category of disorders that may affect the activities of the brain and nervous system (such as speech, listening, vision, perception, and thinking) caused by disruption to the other areas of the developing brain

- The critical optic nerve is impaired by high pressure.

Black Eye (conjunctivitis)-conjunctive skin inflammation

1.4 Effects of drugs on the nervous system

- Alcohol-depressant of the central nervous system-cell membranes are extremely alcohol permeable, and they can spread into virtually all body tissues until they are in the bloodstream. It is consumed through the intestine such that it passes through the blood rapidly and speeds down the nervous system process

- Caffeine-functions as a central nervous system stimulant

- Caffeine suppresses up to 10 hours of melatonin and stimulates adrenaline as well. Melatonin is closely related to healthy sleep, while adrenaline is the warning neurotransmitter.

- Nicotine – minimal amounts of nicotine have a calming effect on the central nervous system– it is highly addictive nicotine effects on the brain that enhance the production of pleasure-related neurotransmitters. The brain adapts rapidly to the repeated use of nicotine by lowering the amount of activated neurotransmitters. To order to avoid the feeling of pain associated with the opioid removal, the user must continue to use nicotine. During nicotine withdrawal, irritability and anxiety often occur.

- Cannabis-THC, the main active agent of cannabis, binds to nerve cell membranes with protein receptors in the central nervous system. THC initiates a chemical reaction after its binding to nerve cells, which causes the various effects of the use of marijuana. One consequence is the repression of memory and learning areas in the brain (called hippocampus).

Chapter 2: Cranial Nerves

The cranial nerves are set of12 brain nerves. Every nerve has a particular meaning or movement feature. The function of cranial nerves is visual, motor, or both, so that a person can see, feel, and hear through visual cranial nerves. Cranial motor nerves help to regulate the contraction of the muscles in the head and back.

Growing nerve has a number that represents its function and its location in the brain. Scientists use I–XII Roman numerals to mark the brain's cranial nerves.

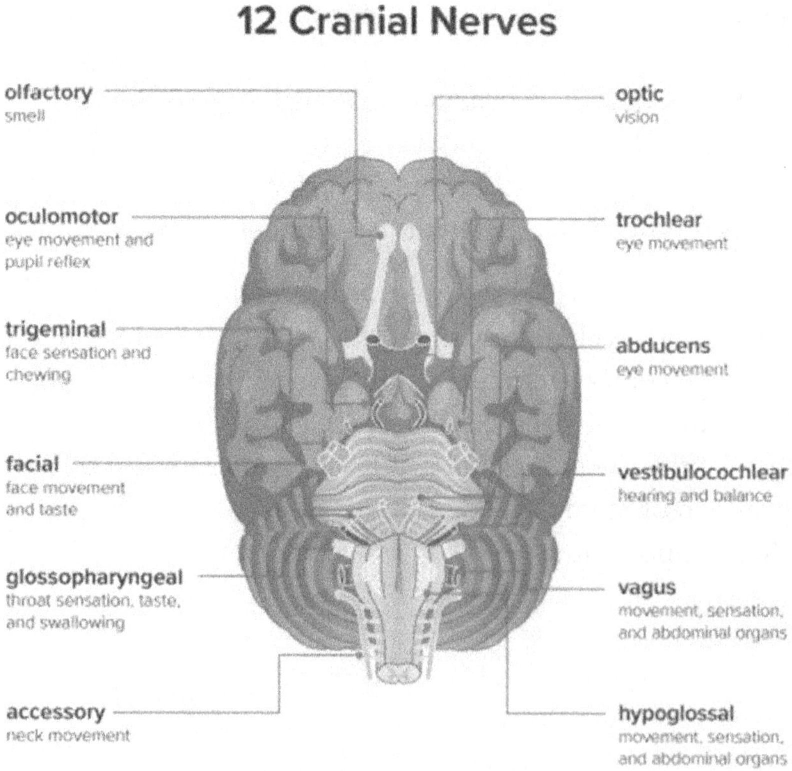

The 12 Cranial Nerves

I. Olfactory Nerve

The olfactory nerve sends knowledge about the sense of scent of a human to the brain.

When a human inhales fragrant chemicals, olfactory receptors transmit signals through the cranial cavity inside the nasal passage, which flies to the olfactory bulb.

Specialized olfactory neurons and nerve fibers, which travel through the olfactory duct, cross other nerves. The olfactory tract then moves to the front lobe and other brain regions, which include the memory and writing of various smells

II. Optic Nerve

The optic nerve transmits knowledge about the vision of a human to the brain. The light, which includes rods and cones, reaches the retina as it approaches the eye. They are picture receptors that translate light signals into brain visual information.

Cones in the main retina are involved in color vision. Rods in the posterior eye are located that include non-color vision. Such photoreceptors carry signal impulses to form the optic nerve via the nerve cells. Many of the optic nerve fibers are converted into a system called the optic chiasm. The perceptual pathway connects to the primary visual cortex at the back of the brain in the occipital lobe. The occipital cortex is where sensory input is treated by the brain.

III. Oculomotor Nerve

The oculomotor nerve helps regulate the eye's muscle movements. Most muscles that control the eyeball and upper eyepiece, known as extraocular muscles, are regulated by the oculomotor nerve. The oculomotor nerve also supports the unintended operation of the eye: As light reflects, the sphincter muscle spontaneously constricts the pupil. The muscle relaxes as the shadow allows the light to penetrate. The ciliary muscles allow the lens to adjust to short and long vision. It immediately occurs when a human looks at things close or far.

IV. Trochlear Nerve

The trochlear nerve also assists in the development of the head. Like the oculomotor nerve, the trochlear nerve arises from the midbrain. It activates the superior oblique contralateral muscle that causes the eye to look inward and inward.

V. Trigeminal Nerve

The trigeminal nerve is the main cranial nerve with both motor and sensory functions. These motor functions allow a human to knock and clamp their teeth to make the muscles sound at the tympanic membrane of the brain.

The sensory section of the visual system includes three parts linking the sensory receptors: the ophthalmic part provides feeling to areas of the body, including the cornea, your mucosa in the nose and skin on your face, your eyelid and your forehead. The maxilla part lets you notice the middle third of your forehead, nose, upper teeth, and lower eyes. The lower third of the neck, the voice, the mucosa in the mouth, and lower teeth are sensed by the mandibular portion. Trigeminal neuralgia is a common trigeminal nerve condition that can cause extreme pain and facial tics.

VI. Abducens Nerve

The abducens nerve also helps regulate the movement of the hand. This lets the lateral rectal muscle, one of the extraocular muscles, see beyond. The abducens nerve starts in the brain stem pons and passes into a region known as the canal of Dorello, travels into the cavernous sinus, and ends in the ostrich's lateral rectal muscle.

VII. Facial Nerve

The facial nerve has both visual and motor functions. The facial nerve consists of four nuclei, which act in different ways: muscle movements that create the lacrimal, sub-maxillary, and submandibular movement of facial expression; sensations of a sensation of the taste of the external ear. The four nuclei arise from pons and medulla and combine to travel to the geniculate ganglion. Bell's paralysis is a common facial nerve condition, which induces on one side of the facial paralysis and likely taste loss.

VIII. Vestibulocochlear Nerve

The vestibulocochlear nerve is involved in the hearing and equilibrium of a human.

The nerve comprises two components: the vestibular nerve aids the body in detecting changes in the head's location in terms of gravity. This knowledge is used by the body to preserve equilibrium. Hearing stimulates the cochlear nerve. In response to sound, sensitive inner hair cells and the basilar membrane vibrate and determine the rate and amplitude of the sound. Such fibers join in the pons and exit the skull in the temporal bone in the inner acoustic tissue.

IX. Glossopharyngeal nerve

The motor and sensory functions of the glossopharyngeal nerve. The sensory feature is told by the mouth, tonsils, middle eye, and back of the tongue. This also includes the sense of flavor on the tongue's back. The motor movement pushes the stylopharyngeus, which is a muscle that will narrow and expand the throat. The glossopharyngeal nerve starts with the oblongata medulla in the brain and exits the skull by the jugular foramen leading to the tympanic nerve.

X. Vagus nerve

Vagus nerve has a number of motor, sensory, and parasympathetic functions. The sensory component gives the outside of the ear, the mouth, the heart, and the abdominal organs the feeling. It also plays a part in the sense of taste. The motor part pushes the mouth and the palate gently. The parasympathetic mechanism controls the movement of the heart and instills the airway, kidneys, and gastrointestinal muscles into the smooth tissue. The vagus nerve is longest cranial nerve it starts in the medulla and enters the abdomen. Physicians treat different disorders, including autism, insomnia, and anxiety, using vaguely-nervous relaxation therapy.

XI. Accessory Nerve

Some of the muscles in the neck are motorized by the attachment nerve: it regulates the sternocleidomastoid and the trapezius that allows a human to twist, stretch, and flex the neck and shoulders. The peripheral nerve is spinal and cranial. The spinal portion starts in the spinal cord and passes through the foramen magnum into the skull. It enters the cranial component from there leaves skull with central carotid artery. The cranial part of the peripheral nerve and the vagus nerve is combined.

XII. Hypoglossal Nerve

The hypoglossal nerve is an artificial nerve supplying the muscles of the tongue. The hypoglossal nerve emerges from the medulla. Hypoglossal nerve disorders can cause tongue paralysis, most often in one side.

Summary: The twelve cranial nerves are set of nerves which originate in the brain and provide the head and neck with motor or sensory functions—the distinctive anatomical features and functions of each cranial nerve.

Doctors may diagnose neurological or mental disorders by examining the functions of the cranial nerve.

Chapter 3: Vagus Nerve

Among the 12 pairs among cranial nerves arising from the skull, the vagus nerve is the largest and most complex. It transmits information from or to tissues and organs elsewhere in the body. The name ' vagus' comes from the Latin word for' wandering,' since the nerve wanders in the arm, chest, and abdomen from the brain into animals. Sometimes named the 10th cranial nerve or cranial nerve X.

3.1 What is a Vagus Nerve?

The vagus nerve is connected to the body by two bunches of tactile nerve cells. It helps the brain to track and collect information about different functions of the body. The vagus nerve and its associated parts deliver various nervous system functions. The vagus nerve functions relate to the parasympathetic and sympathetic portions of the autonomic nervous system.

The nerve is responsible for many sensory functions and for motor information in the body. It is ultimately part of a system that connects the brain, the body, the heart, the lungs, and the abdomen.

3.2 Anatomy of Vagus Nerve

The vagus nerve (also referred to as the 10th cranial nerve, CN X) is a very long nerve beginning in the brain tube and running across the neck and chest and abdomen. When both motor and sensory information are present, the heart contains innervation, large blood vessels, airways, kidneys, esophagus, stomach, intestines. Although there are two vagus nerves, the left and the right, doctors generally refer to them as a "vagus nerve." It plays a critical role in controlling the heart rate and maintaining a proper gastrointestinal tract. The vagus nerves also transmit sensory input back to the brain from the internal organs

3.3 Functions of Vagus Nerve

The vagus nerve has different functions. The vagus nerve has four main functions: sensory: mouth, back, lungs, and abdomen.

Special sensory: gives the tongue a flavor sensation.

Motor Includes communication mechanisms for swallowing and communicating of the muscles in the arm.

Parasympathetic: Essential for the regulation of the digestive tract, respiration, and heart rate.

The tasks can be further categorized into seven groups. Another is to regulate the nervous system. There are two regions of the nervous system: sympathetic and parasympathetic. The nice side increases alertness, stamina, blood pressure, heart rate, and respiration.

The vagus nerve's parasympathetic side decreases alertness, blood pressure, and pulse rate and promotes calmness, relaxation, and digestion. As a consequence, the vagus nerve also leads to defecation, urination, and sexual arousal.

Many vagus nerve effects include coordination between the brain and intestines: the vagus nerve transmits data from the intestines into the brain.

Deep breathing relaxation: the diaphragm interacts with the vagus nerve. An individual feels more relaxed with deep breaths.

Reducing inflammation: The vagus nerve sends certain areas of the body an anti-inflammatory message.

Reduction of blood pressure and pulse rate: if the vagus nerve becomes overactive, it will hinder the pulse from circulating enough blood throughout the body. Excessive vagus nerve activation, in some cases, can lead to a lack of consciousness and organ injury.

Fear control: The ambiguous nerve transfers information from the intestines to the brain, which is associated with the regulation of pain, anxiety, and terror–thus the term "good feeling."

Probably the main importance of the vagus nerve is the body's largest parasympathetic nerve, which provides the head, back, chest, and abdominal parasympathetic fibers.

Vasovagal Reflex

The vagus nerve has a function for coughing reflex (and the cough reflex when the ear canal is stimulated). It is responsible for increasing the pulse rate, suppressing breathing, maintaining the blood pressure, activating the peristalsis of the gastrointestinal tract, and managing the vocal sound. This reflection can be caused by stomach illness or by discomfort, anxiety, or sudden stress. Some individuals are especially susceptible to vasovagal reflexes, which may induce a lack of consciousness by blood pressure and heart rate changes— a disorder called "vasovagal syncope." Abnormal nerve activity is often seen in certain medical conditions, especially dysautonomia.

Stimulating the nerve may have beneficial effects (such as preventing SVT episodes or hiccups. And can assist clinicians in treating other forms of heart whisperings. When using the Valsalva technique, vagal stimulation can be done very quickly.

The right vagus nerve supports the sinus node, and its activation will contribute to bradycardia sinus. The left vagus nerve supplies the AV node, and activation of the node will produce a type of cardiac obstruction. The Valsalva maneuver will relieve several kinds of SVT by creating a temporary heart barrier.

3.4 The Vagus nerve in medical therapy

Owing to the many essential roles of the vagus nerve, medical research has been involved in medical diagnosis for decades by using vagus nerve stimulation or vagus nerve blocking. For decades, the vagotomy procedure became the basis of treatment for peptic ulcer disease (cutting off the vagus nerve) because it decreased the amount of peptic acid released by the stomach. Nonetheless, the vagotomy has a variety of adverse effects, and with more efficient therapy available, the use of electronic stimulators (essentially modified pacemakers) to continuously activate the vagal nerve in an effort to cure various medical conditions nowadays is much less prevalent.5 Such devices (generally referred to as vagus nerve stimulators or VNS devices) were widely used to treat patients with extreme medications- refractive epilepsy. VNS treatment is also often used to treat refractive depression 6. And if a hammer appears like a rock, businesses using VNS tools evaluate their use in many other disorders, including asthma, migraines, tinnitus, fibromyalgia, and weight loss.

3.5 Vagus nerve stimulation

Vagus nerve stimulation is a surgical technique used to treat a variety of disorders. This can be achieved manually or by electric pulses. Clinical trials have tested the effectiveness of vagus nerve stimulation. Consequently, two separate conditions were approved in the United States Food and Drug Administration (FDA).

Epilepsy

It consists of a tiny electronic tool in the chest of a human, equivalent to a pacemaker. Through the unit to the slight nerve passes a thin wire known as a thread. The system is put under general anesthetics by surgery in the body. It then delivers electric shocks to the brain via the vagus nerve at frequent intervals during the day to lessen the severity of the hallucinations or even to interrupt them.

The side effects of vagus nerve stimulation include thick, rough changes of voice, sore throat, shortness of breath, low heart rate, painful trouble swallowing, stomach pain, or nausea. Those taking this type of medication should also inform a doctor if they have complications, so this can avoid or mitigate these symptoms.

The following symptoms have also been shown to help: Rapid cycling bipolar disorder, anxiety disorders, and Alzheimer's disease

Further research and considerations

For nearly every organ in the body in the vagus nerve, researchers see how relaxation will improve certain disorders. Such disorders include rheumatoid arthritis inflammation and cardiac insufficiency inflammation from diabetes mellitus intractable diabetic hiccups irregular heart rhythm inflammation from Crohn's disease. A report in 2016 showed that vago nert stimulation might help minimize symptoms in the U.S. in cases and rheumatoid arthritis, which affects 1.3 million adults. Individuals that had not responded to other therapies registered substantial changes without evidence of serious adverse effects. This has been considered a major advance in the treatment of rheumatoid arthritis and other infectious disorders such as Crohn's, Parkinson's, or Alzheimer's.

Chapter 4: Vagus Nerve and Epilepsy

Epilepsy typically requires frequent seizures. These seizures occur due to electrical activity disturbances in the brain, which temporarily interrupt the communication processes between brain cells.

Epilepsy is defined in the Centers for Disease Control and Prevention (CDC) as "a serious brain disease that triggers repeated seizures."

4.1. Symptoms of Epilepsy

Recurring seizures are the primary symptom of epilepsy. If, however, one or more symptoms of this disorder arise, one will seek medical treatment because epilepsy may indicate: convulsion without fever, brief blackouts or confused memory, occasional fainting spells, during which they lose the control of the intestines or blades, often accompanied by intense fatigue transient inability to respond unexpectedly to orders and questions

The following problems may trigger similar effects to those above, such that certain people may associate them for seizures, such as seizure-like signs, fainting narcolepsy, frequent cataplexy bouts in sleep, severe body fatigue with sleep disturbances, heart panic attacks, a rare psychological illness under which someone has plunged into a state in flight.

4.2. Treatment

For certain cases of epilepsy, there is actually no treatment. Antiepileptic medications (AEDs) can be administered by a doctor to help avoid seizures. Many other future treatments include chemotherapy, nerve stimulation, or a strict diet if such medications do not function.

The goal of doctors is to avoid further seizures. It also aims to avoid adverse effects so that the patient can live a healthy and prosperous life.

AEDs

According to the American Epilepsy Society, AEDs occur in about 60–70 percent of cases to better control seizures. The type of epilepsy a person has decides which medication the doctor prescribes.

The bulk of AEDs are taken by hand. Popular epilepsy medicines include:

- **Valproic acid**
- **Carbamazepine**
- **Lamotrigine**
- **Levetiracetam**

Several medicines may avoid seizures in one, but not in another individual. Sometimes, even when a person chooses the right drug, determining the optimal dosage can take some time.

Surgery

A psychiatrist may consider prescribing epilepsy surgery if at least two medications have not been successful in stopping the seizures. A 2013 Swedish study showed that almost seven years after the epilepsy procedure, 62% of adults and 50% of children with epilepsy had no seizures.

According to the NIDS, other surgical choices include lobectomy: During this operation, a surgeon must cut the part of the brain in which a seizure occurs. It is the first form of surgery for epilepsy.

Multiple subpial transections: a surgeon may make multiple cuts during this operation to restrict epilepsy to one region of the brain.

Corpus Callosotomy: a surgeon must break synaptic connections between the two brain sections. In this way, seizures do not move from one side of the brain to the other.

Hemispherectomy: In serious situations, a surgeon can need to remove one half of the brain cortex from the hemisphere.

In certain cases, the duration and severity of the seizures can be decreased. Nevertheless, antiseizure treatment is also necessary to use for many years after the procedure. Another choice is to insert a system in the chest to stimulate the vagus in the lower throat. This system provides an electric shock to the brain in order to help prevent seizures.

Diet

Diet can help prevent seizures. According to a research published in the journal Neurology in 2014, extremely fat, low carbohydrate diets will support epileptic children and adults.

Five research in the study used the ketogenic diet, while a tweaked Atkins diet was used by another five. Typical beef, ham, avocados, cheese, almonds, fish, and other fruits and vegetables are included in such diets. The study showed that 32 percent of research participants who follow the ketogenic diet and 29 percent of study participants who follow the modified Atkins diet reported at least a 50% reduction in seizure regularity. Nevertheless, it was impossible for many people to sustain such diets.

For certain cases, different diets can be useful, although more work is required to prove it.

4.3. Causes of Epilepsy

Messaging mechanisms regulate any feature of the human body inside the brain. Epilepsy occurs as a result of a disturbance of the system that may arise from brain damage.

For certain cases, the precise cause would not be clear to health care practitioners. Any individuals inherit genetic conditions that are more likely to cause epilepsy. Many causes that may raise the risk include head injuries, such as from a car crash brain disorder, including stroke and cancers infectious disorders such as viral encephalitis cysticercosis AIDS prenatal disability or brain impairment that happens before birth conditions, including autism and neurofibromatosis According to the CDC, epilepsy is most prone to degenerate.

Was epilepsy widespread?

In 2015, the CDC estimated that about 1.2 percent of the U.S. population was afflicted by epilepsy. That's around 3.4 million people, including 3 million adults and 470,000 babies.

World Health Organization (WHO) reports that about 50 million individuals worldwide are afflicted by epilepsy.

Doctors may often recognize a person's cause of seizures. There are two major forms of epilepsy, depending on how doctors can identify the cause: idiopathic or cryptogenic: there is no clear cause unless the doctor is unable to ascertain the cause.

Symptomatic: The psychiatrist knows what the cause is. There are also three descriptors of seizures— partial, primary, and primary secondary — depending on the region of the brain the epilepsy originates in.

The perception of a person during a seizure will depend on the region of the brain affected and how quickly and rapidly the electrical stimulation in the brain extends from that initial location.

Partial epilepsy

A partial coma happens in one part of a person's brain when the epileptic disorder happens. Two subtypes of partial seizure exist Simple partial seizure: the person is conscious during this form of seizure. You are still mindful of their surroundings, in most situations, particularly though the attack is occurring.

Complex partial seizure: The seizure impairs a person's consciousness during this form. Generally, they won't recall the attack. If they do, their knowledge of it is going to be unclear.

A widespread epilepsy happens where the epileptic disorder involves all brain halves. Usually, the person will lose consciousness when the seizure is underway.

There are many subtypes of

- Generalized seizure, including tonic-clonic seizures: Maybe the best-known type of generalized seizure, tonic-clonic seizures, and cause lack of control, body trembling, and shaking. Such grand mal seizures have been called by physicians since.
- Absence seizures: Previously known as petit mal seizures, these include brief lapses of consciousness in which the patient seems to be looking into space. Absence seizures also respond well to therapy.
- Tonic seizures: Muscles become rigid in tonic seizures, and the person can fall.

- Atonic seizures: A lack of muscle tone triggers a sudden drop in the adult.
- Clonic seizures: This subtype is responsible for rhythmic, jerking activity, sometimes in the face or in one arm or leg.
- Myoclonic seizures: This subtype induces a rapid movement or twitch between the upper body and hands.
- Secondary generalized seizure: A secondary generalized seizure occurs as the epileptic disorder starts as a partial seizure but is extending to all brain halves. The person will lose consciousness as this seizure progresses.

4.4. Diagnosis

To diagnose epilepsy, a psychiatrist must review the medical history of a person and the symptoms they have encountered, including a summary and list of previous seizures.

They may also apply for testing to determine the type of epilepsy and the number of seizures that the patient has. The specialist will be able to recommend treatment options depending on these tests, such as anti-seizure drugs.

A specialist may be able to diagnose epilepsy through various types of imaging testing. Such measures include: an EEG to check for suspicious CT and MRI brain waves scans, to diagnose cancers or other anatomical abnormalities functional MRI scans that can distinguish natural and pathological brain activity in different regions of single-photon emission CT scans that can determine the initial site of a brain seizure Is epilepsy genetic?

Approximately 70–80% of cases of epilepsy arise as a consequence of inheritance, according to one 2015 study analysis. A scientific study in 2017 related more than 900 genes to epilepsy. As more experiments take place, the number continues to grow.

Genes may specifically contribute to autism, brain abnormalities that may lead to seizures or other seizure-causing genetic disorders. In certain cases, genetic traits are inherited. However, in individuals without a family history of the disease, other genetic defects can also cause epilepsy. A psychiatrist may sometimes call for genetic testing to determine the cause of epilepsy, which can use electrical waves to detect abnormalities in brain function. The doctor may also use blood tests to determine any underlying conditions that may cause epilepsy. Neurological tests can also help a psychiatrist assess the type of epilepsy the patient has.

Triggers

Seizures can result from a number of factors. One research in 2014 reported stress, sleep deprivation, and exhaustion among 104 participants as the most frequent causes. Flickering lights and excessive alcohol intake can cause seizures.

Stress is a frequent cause of seizures, but it's unclear why. This mechanism was the subject of 2016 work in the journal Science Signaling. The team found that the reaction to stress in the brain behaved better in epileptic rats than in those without.

The study has shown that instead, the enzyme, which normally suppresses brain activity in response to stress, has increased activity, which can aid in seizures?

Epilepsy vs. seizures

The main symptom of epilepsy is convulsions. Of addition, epilepsy is described by Johns Hopkins Medicine as having "two or more unprovoked seizures." Many patients may have a single seizure, or they may have seizures not triggered by epilepsy. Doctors might even misdiagnose non- epileptic seizures as epilepsy. Non-epileptic seizures, however, are not caused by irregular electrical activity in the brain. The causes of these can be physical, neurological, or mental. There are also different types of seizures that can vary among people suffering from epilepsy. For example, in two people with epilepsy, the diagnosis can look different.

For this reason, the CDC defines autism as a condition of the spectrum.

Is Epilepsy a disability?

The Americans with Disabilities Act (ADA) forbids violence against disabled people, including epilepsy. This happens whether the person is able to use medicine or surgery to treat their seizures or not. Individuals with epilepsy have some workplace rights under the ADA, including the following: Employers should not inquire about the medical needs of work seekers, including epilepsy.

Unless they need a reasonable accommodation during the application period, job applicants do not need to tell an employer that they have epilepsy. Employers may not revoke a job offer if the person is able to perform the primary job functions. People with epilepsy may be eligible for disability benefits, according to the Social Security Administration. It requires people to record the nature and severity of their epilepsy by taking all the prescribed medications.

4.5. Warning devices

Many apps can control seizures and alert parents, hopefully improving recovery and avoiding sudden accidental epileptic death (SUDEP).

Another such multimodality unit, the Night-watch, was linked to an Emfit bed sensor by a small 2018 test involving 28 patients, the findings of which appeared in the journal Neurology. The Night-watch recorded 85 percent of all serious seizures compared to the bed sensor's 21 percent. Every 25 nights, it has missed only one significant attack.

According to one report in 2017, almost 70 percent of SUDEP cases occur during the night. This means that the use of specific nighttime alarm systems may be of possible value.

Is it infectious?

Everyone can develop epilepsy, but it is not infectious. A literature analysis in 2016 examined several misconceptions and stereotypes around epilepsy, namely the mistaken assumption that epilepsy would spread amongst individuals

The writers of the study state that those of lower rates of schooling and social background had a large incidence of myths, as did someone who did not encounter any persons of epilepsy.

As a consequence, therapies and other outreach initiatives can be helpful in reducing epileptic distress and improving awareness of the disorder.

4.6. Prognosis

Epilepsy will affect a person's life in multiple ways, and the future may depend on various factors.

Occasionally, hallucinations can be fatal, depending on the circumstances. Nevertheless, other patients with epilepsy use anti-seizure drugs to treat their seizures.

The suspected association between seizures and brain injury needs to be verified by further studies. Seizures can lead to drowning, falling, car crashes, or other fatal injuries. Although it is uncommon, it may also occur at SUDEP.

Cases of SUDEP typically occur during or immediately following a seizure. For instance, the seizure could cause the person to go too long without breathing, or it could lead to heart failure. SUDEP's exact cause is unknown, but a 2018 animal study suggested that it could be explained by acid reflux. SUDEP did not occur in the rats, which the researchers examined after blocking acid from entering the esophagus. Though, it's not obvious if this has any significance to humans. People are at greater risk of SUDEP if they have had epilepsy for many years, or if they have regular seizures, according to the CDC. Following these steps can help to reduce the risk of SUDEP: taking all doses of anti-seizure medication limiting alcohol intake to get enough Regular sleep medication may also help prevent epileptic status, a condition in which seizures last longer than 5 minutes.

A research carried out in 2016 showed that treating the epileptic condition within 30 minutes decreased the risk of death.

Will the seizures carry on?

A research review in the journal Brain in 2013 indicated that 65–85 percent of people might experience long-term seizure remission. Nevertheless, convulsions with an apparent origin are more likely to continue. Many factors that affect the likelihood of recovery include exposure to a medical reaction to other health conditions a person may have, with proper use of anti-seizure drugs, most people with epilepsy may be able to control their seizures.

Could epilepsy cause brain injury?

Analysis into whether seizures can induce brain damage or not has provided mixed results.

A 2018 study looked at postoperative brain tissue from people with recurrent seizures. The investigators found no markers of brain damage in people with certain types of epilepsy. Several other studies, however, have shown that serious, long-lasting seizures may cause brain damage. For example, one study in 2013 showed that seizures might lead to anomalies in the brain, with epileptic status causing permanent brain lesions. Many studies have explored neurological changes in children as they age, with or without epilepsy. Results suggest a correlation between epilepsy and worse cognitive outcomes. It is uncertain, however, whether: epilepsy causes the condition, a related structural change causes both epilepsy and disability antiepileptic medications to have an effect.

Other consequences

Epilepsy will impair different facets of a person's life, including their: attitudes and mental, emotional learning, and interpersonal capacity to learn and function. The extent of the impact on these areas of life will depend primarily on the frequency and severity of their seizures.

Life expectancy in patients with epilepsy Scientists at the University of Oxford and University College London, also in the United Kingdom, found that individuals with epilepsy are 11 times more likely to suffer early mortality than someone without it.

When the individual also has a mental health condition, the risk tends to be greater. Suicide, injuries, and robberies were blamed for 15.8 percent of early deaths. Many people affected by these also had been diagnosed with a disease of mental health.

Lead researcher Seena Fazel says, "Our findings have important public health consequences, because about 70 million people worldwide have epilepsy, and emphasize that proper evaluation and diagnosis of psychiatric conditions because part of routine tests of [people] with epilepsy may help to minimize the risk of premature death in these patients." "Our report," he continues, "also emphasizes the value of epilepsy. According to a 2017 literature analysis in NeuroToxicology, these causes include age, with new events emerging most commonly in young children and older adults with brain trauma and hereditary cancers and family history drug use perinatal causes such as stroke and infections of the central nervous system premature birth, such as bacterial meningitis, viral encephalitis.

Can it be cured?

There is currently no cure for epilepsy, but it is usually possible for people with the condition to manage their symptoms. According to the WHO, antiseizure drugs will decrease their seizure frequency and duration by up to 70 percent in patients with epilepsy. For two years without a stroke, about half of all patients with epilepsy will be able to avoid taking drugs. For certain cases, surgery can also limit or remove epilepsy, where there is the ineffectiveness of medications.

That can have benefits in the long term. For one survey in 2018, 47 percent of participants reported no serious seizures five years after surgery, and after ten years, 38 percent reported the same.

4.7. Prevention

The WHO states that about 25 per cent of cases involving epilepsy can be avoided. By taking these steps, individuals may decrease the likelihood of contracting epilepsy: wearing a helmet while riding a bicycle or motorcycle, helping prevent head injury accessing perinatal treatment, avoiding epilepsy from birth accidents, reducing risk factors for stroke and cardiac failure, which may trigger brain harm that results in healthy health and prevention measures to stop epilepsy

A 2015 study analysis in the journal Seizure also indicated that regular physical activity could help prevent epilepsy development and decrease how often seizures occur. Both forms of epilepsy are not preventable. Taking the above measures may, however, help to reduce the risk.

4.8. Complications

Seizures can lead to adverse outcomes such as death or car collisions, depending on the situation. Long duration seizures, or epileptic state, can also result in brain injury or death.

People with epilepsy are eight times more likely to experience certain other chronic conditions like diabetes, asthma, heart disease, and depression than people without it. Some of those things might also trigger seizures. Certain risks can arise because of the side effects of antiseizure medications. For example, one study in 2015 found that 9.98

percent of people taking the lamotrigine (Lamictal) antiseizure drug developed a skin rash. Many AEDs, like phenytoin (Dilantin) and phenobarbital, can also cause a rash. The rash normally vanishes as soon as the person starts taking the drug. Nevertheless, 0.8 percent of adults - 1.3 percent developed a severe rash that could be fatal.

4.9. Vagus nerve stimulation for epilepsy

Vagus nerve stimulation (VNS) is a special therapy for epilepsy in that it requires an external mechanism to cure a condition that is directly linked to neurological events happening within the brain. An understanding of the sensory anatomy and physiology of the vagus nerve is important to understand how vagus nerve stimulation can be used to stop seizures. The analysis explores the peripheral features of the vagus nerve, with an overview of which fibers and branches are involved in generating such antiepileptic symptoms, along with hypotheses on the ability to enhance the treatment.

Introduction

A series of experiments performed by Zabara demonstrated that vagus nerve stimulation (VNS) could be used to avoid experimentally triggered dog seizures. These results led directly to the development of a commercial VNS system, first clinically implanted by Penry and his colleagues in 1988. The European Community approved the use of VNS for seizures in 1994 after several broad clinical studies, followed by the Food and Drug Administration (FDA) approval in the USA in 1997. VNS is widely used as an adjunctive therapy for medication-resistant epilepsy in more than 40,000 patients and is, as of this date, the only FDA-approved device-related treatment for refractory seizures.

VNS provides a lower-risk surgery with fewer complications compared to other neurosurgical procedures in which the target is surgically removed. The procedure requires inserting helical electrodes on the left cervical vagus nerve, with occasional stimulation being received by a subcutaneously implanted neurocybernetic prosthesis throughout the upper arm.

The stimulation parameters vary; however, studies indicate that optimum seizure security can be obtained with stimuli provided at 20–30 Hz on a periodic basis. Most patients are usually stimulated at 30 Hz, with a continuous 30-second stimulus interval on and5-minute off. Clinical studies find the system to decrease the occurrence of severe partial seizures in the majority of patients studied, with 20–40 percent of patients experiencing a drop in seizure frequency by more than 50%. The number of responses increases over time, although the number of antiepileptic medicines (AEDs) required to sustain adequate control of seizures reduces after VNS.

VNS side-effects are typically limited to coughing and/or speech heaviness. These side effects can be produced uniformly with the adequate amplitude of VNS or the width of the pulse, but they are not required for the therapeutic response. Such side effects are often elicited when the VNS settings are changed but are typically temporary or can be removed immediately by the appropriate VNS parameters.

VNS is a special therapy for epilepsy in that it requires a secondary method to treat a condition that is completely While it is often said that the therapeutic mechanisms of VNS have not been fully elucidated, it is obvious from numerous studies that activation of vagal afferents by electrical stimulation, directly and indirectly, affects well-defined seizure-related circuitry within the brain.

Knowledge of the peripheral structure and physiology of the vagus nerve and its main branches is crucial to understanding how activation of the vagus nerve can be used to interrupt seizures. This analysis addresses only the peripheral features of the vagus nerve, describing what fibers and branches are involved in the antiepileptic activity of VNS. The VNS key processes will be discussed separately.

Vagus nerve anatomy

Vagus is the Latin word for "wandering." The name alludes to the nature of the connections created within the body by the branches of this nerve. The vagus nerve is a combination of afferent sensory and efferent motor fibers that migrate together in a shared direction, each with its own origin, destination, and the threshold for activation.

Despite the emphasis put in most introductory texts on the motor effects of the vagus nerve, the sensory afferents greatly outnumber the motor efferents, containing roughly 65–80 percent of all vagal fibers. The vagus nerve comprises branchial and visceral motor components, as well as visceral and general sensory components. Some of the sensory afferents perform brain information about the internal environment, while other motor efferents supply the organs with parasympathetic outflow. Such fibers leave or enter the medulla from both sides in 8–10 rootlets, and coalesce into a nerve trunk going through the jugular foramen. The vagus innervates all of the main thoracic and intestinal organs, supplying profuse brain/body connectivity.

Efferent fibers

The vagus nerve branchial motor nerves innervate the neck and face skeletal muscles. For such fibers, the cell bodies are found in the unclear nucleus. The fibers of three primary branches leave the vagal root. The pharyngeal branch includes much of the pharynx and soft palate striate muscles motor innervation, and a part of the tongue. The upper laryngeal branch includes the larynx's inferior constrictor and cricothyroid muscles, and the pharyngeal plexus. The recurring laryngeal branch leaves the vagal trunk more distal than the others and takes a somewhat circuitous path to innervate all of the laryngeal muscles, except the cricothyroid. The recurring branch of the left laryngeal crosses under the aorta while the right branch crosses under the subclavian artery.

Visceral motor preganglionic fibers reside in the dorsal motor nucleus of the vagus, with the exception of cardiomotor neurons tend to reside in the nucleus ambiguus, preganglionic fibers synapse on ganglia supplying parasympathetic innervation with extensive cardiopulmonary and gastrointestinal processes, and pharyngeal and laryngeal mucosal glands. The above is protected by the divisions of the pharyngeal, superior laryngeal, and recurring laryngeal, respectively, following the directions mentioned above, The branches of the pulmonary, esophageal, and cardiac motor exit the vagal trunks inside the neck and thorax at different stages, and synapse into ganglia inside their target. Pulmonary branches exit the trunk in the thoracic cavity and along with the fibers from the sympathetic trunk ganglia form anterior and posterior pulmonary plexuses. The bronchial smooth muscles are innervated by these pulmonary branches. Esophageal plexuses are also developed over the entire length of the esophagus from vagal branches inside the thoracic cavity. Such fibers know the esophagus ' smooth muscles. Several branches on either side support the nucleus: the upper and lower cervical cardiac branches that leave the main trunk in humans at the point of the thyroid gland approximately, and the thoracic, cardiac branch that leaves when the vagal trunk crosses past the neck. The left and right cardiac motor fibers invert the heart asymmetrically, with fibers from the left vagus nerve supplying the atrioventricular (AV) node (causing decremental conduction) and those from the right vagus nerve introducing the sinoatrial (SA) node (reducing the rate of depolarization and producing bradycardia). It is estimated that 75% of visceral motor fibers in subdiaphragmatic organs are present in the vagal trunk project.

Afferent fibers

The vast majority of vagal fibers are small unmyelinated afferents. Most of these unmyelinated afferents are visceral sensory fibers that carry information

from the stomach, intestines, liver, pancreas, and spleen. Nearly all visceral sensory are visceral fibers. A small percentage of these fibers can also bear visceral pain information from the heart, esophagus, and trachea. Larger myelinated vagal afferents moving from baroreceptors located in the aortic arch and pulmonary airways, and also from chemoreceptors located in the aortic bone, join these fibers at the cervical level. Stimulation of these cardiac and pulmonary fibers can contribute to reflex breathing disturbance (Hering- Breuer Reflex), bradycardia, and vasoconstrictions.

The general sensory fibers have much less extensive area than the massive sensory visceral system. General sensory fibers bring information from the ear and portions of the pharynx and larynx to the touch, pain, and temperature. Auricular branch fibers, which internalize the pinna and the auditory canal, penetrate the jugular (superior vagal) ganglion directly without entering the vagal spine. By comparison, general pharynx and larynx sensory fibers follow the motor fibers in either the upper laryngeal or repetitive laryngeal branches, with their cell bodies in the nodose (lower vagal) ganglion. Eventually, all the general sensory fibers synapse inside the trigeminal nerve spinal nucleus.

4.10. Vagal fibers involved in the anti-epileptic effects of vagus nerve stimulation

Understanding the position of a VNS electrode on the vagal trunk and identifying side effects triggered by VNS can provide valuable information about the vagal branches and fiber forms that are activated during therapeutic VNS. The VNS electrodes are located on the left vagal cervical spine, about 8 cm above the clavicle. Except for the occasional laryngeal node, VNS is unlikely to trigger the auricular, laryngeal, and pharyngeal divisions when they exit the proximal main trunk to the VNS electrodes. The same can be said of the upper and lower cardiac divisions of the cervix. Nevertheless, the majority of the vagal branches and fibers mentioned above are present in the trunk at the level of the VNS electrode and may or may not be activated using standard clinical VNS parameters based on the activation threshold, as discussed below.

Large unmyelinated C-fibers make up the bulk of fibers in the cervical vagus nerve, and activation would contribute to a host of health side effects that would include cardiopulmonary and gastrointestinal processes. Furthermore, such side effects are rarely, if ever, reported in patients at therapeutically important VNS thresholds, leading some investigators to conclude that there is definitely no activation of vagal C-fibers. Studies in animals seem to support this idea. Early VNS study in rats suggested that recruiting of vagal C-fibers is required to suppress seizures. In these studies, different parameters of VNS stimulation were used to elicit the potentials of compound activity in anesthetized rats ' isolated vagus nerve. In anesthetized rats, the criteria required to prevent seizures in awake rats evoked a maximum response from A-, B-, and C-fibers in the isolated vagus nerve. Since large myelinated A-fibers and small myelinated B-fibers have much lower thresholds for activation than necessary to suppress seizures in awake rats, it was concluded that activation of these fibers was not sufficient to suppress seizure, and that activation of C-fibers was necessary. Nevertheless, activation in a chronically implanted, wake-up patient causes neural shunting through the body that is not adequately modeled by a single acute preparation of the nerve. Therefore, the stimulus criteria required to elicit seizure repression in awake animals are presumably not equivalent to those used to stimulate C-fibers in the isolated vagus nerve.

The selective and non-invasive destruction of specific types of vagal fibers, thus eliminating the effects of their activation, maybe a preferable method of determining which types of fibers are involved in the suppression of VNS- induced seizures. In one such experiment, rats were pretreated with either capsaicin, a potent C-fibre excitotoxin, or a drug systemically. C-fiber degradation has been verified by measuring the eye's chemosensitivity; a lack of chemosensitivity suggests that pain fibers (principally C-fibers) have been damaged. It then inserted a cuff electrode on the left cervical vagus nerve. Checking VNS' capacity to inhibit generalized seizures with pentylenetetrazole (PTZ) was achieved after two days. Seizure severities were greatly decreased in vehicle-treated rats during VNS compared with baseline severity. Rats consuming capsaicin–thereby killing most C-fibers in the body, including the vagus nerve–did not, given a lack of chemosensitivity, decrease the potency of VNS. Such findings, in line with the clinical observations, show that activation of vagal C-fibers is not required to obtain suppression of VNS-induced seizure; activation of A- and/or B-fibers is sufficient;

Such results are clinically significant because A-and B-fibers have a far lower threshold of activation because opposed to C-fibers, thus decreasing the amount of current required to achieve VNS antiepileptic effects. Lack of C- fibre mobilization is also important as stimulation of these fibers may create a host of undesirable side effects that are not observed in most patients and would have made the therapy unpleasant.

VAGAL BRANCHES INVOLVED IN THE ANTIEPILEPTIC EFFECTS OF VAGUS NERVE STIMULATION

VNS is usually extended only to the left cervical vagal trunk that includes fibers from recurring vagal branches of the laryngeal, cardiopulmonary, and subdiaphragmatic branches. As these branches perform various functions, not all of the branches automatically relate to the suppression of VNS-induced seizure. Nonetheless, evidence suggests that the induction of seizures can be accomplished by activating the smaller vagal branches. In one such study, the ventral (left) subdiaphragmatic vagal branch in rats was implanted with a cuff electrode. VNS or placebo stimulation was added after two days and caused seizures with PTZ. Forty-eight hours later, reciprocal care was provided, so that each rat behaved as its own monitor. Subdiaphragmatic VNS significantly reduced the frequency of epilepsy associated with baseline. This reduction was similar to that observed in previous experiments with cervical VNS, indicating that activation of the subdiaphragmatic vagal branches alone can inhibit seizures. Although selective stimulation of the subdiaphragmatic branch is successful in suppressing seizures, it is impossible to rule out a role for other branches.

Left vs. right-sided vagal nerve stimulation

Kalia and Mesulam observed that the vagus nerve's midline and unpaired viscera innervated by sensory and motor fibers are defined mainly bilaterally. Nearly two-thirds of the projections from paired systems (such as lungs and bronchi) remain ipsilateral, by contrast. Dog experiments indicate that right- sided VNS contributes to a greater degree of bradycardia than left-sided VNS. It is attributed, as discussed above, to the asymmetric innervation of the heart, with right-sided VNS in dogs triggering the cardiac motor efferents in the SA node. It is widely held that right-sided VNS will not be attempted in a therapeutic environment because of these early dog trials. Yes, the labeling approved by the FDA that covers VNS equipment states, "The NCP device is recommended for use only in stimulating the neck region left vagus nerve.

Safety and effectiveness of treatment with the NCP system have not been identified to activate the right vagus nerve. "Luckily, the cervical vagal trunk structure is distinct for dogs and humans. The cervical vagal trunk in which the VNS electrodes are usually mounted in humans does not have the upper or lower cardiac branches, thus mitigating clinically significant cardiac side effects independent of the implant side. About 0.1% of patients implanted with VNS electrodes on the left vagal trunk experience temporary asystole during intraoperative testing. Although surgeons abandon the implant in around half of these patients, no patients have encountered potential cardiac problems if the VNS electrodes are left in place, indicating an association between VNS and intraoperative patients-occur. In addition, a close evaluation of patients receiving VNS has not shown any clinically significant impact on heart function for up to three years. If intraoperative heart problems are observed, owing to human variations, potential causes include irregular electrode positioning, unwanted collateral manipulation of the heart branches, or irregular vagal anatomy.

If right-sided VNS is free, whether it is successful remains the issue. The response in animal models is, yes. In one test, two groups of rats inserted a cuff electrode to the left or right cervical vagus nerve. VNS was started after two days and inserted into PTZ. A blinded observer ranked the maximum seizure level achieved within 15 minutes. Right-sided cervical VNS was found to be as effective in preventing such PTZ-induced seizures in rats as left-sided cervical VNS. In a later research test, anesthetized pigs were inserted on the cervical vagus nerve with a cuff electrode, and then seizures of the spinal cord were caused by a topical penicillin injection. Cervical VNS greatly decreased this seizure occurrence, regardless of whether it was administered to the left or right leg.

It has since been scientifically illustrated in three separate trials. McGregor and colleagues also published a first case study on patients using right-sided VNS. The three patients were infants who had been implanted with a left-sided VNS system due to postoperative infection and had the system explanted. While effectiveness in one of the patients could not be determined because the device was withdrawn prior to implementation, the other two experienced substantial decreases in seizure from left-sided VNS. After multiple efforts to reimplant the equipment on the left side only to fail due to the severity of the infections, the doctors agreed to continue and put the equipment on the right side. The procedures were un incidental; intraoperative lead experiments were administered with no detectable effects on heart function. Subsequent examination of the patients by Holter did not show postoperative heart symptoms triggered by VNS. Two patients showed no detectable effects on respiration; the third experienced exercise-induced reactive airway disease that was unresponsive to the drug. In this case, the right-sided device was explanted, and the respiratory issue was solved. Notably, this was the only patient who struggled to get a successful response to right-sided VNS seizures. Both the first two patients reported substantial declines in epilepsy with right-sided VNS and received therapy without noticeable side effects.

The second right-sided VNS clinical case concerned another infant who first received left-sided VNS and who was eventually excluded due to postoperative infection. A right-sided solution was introduced, leading to severe fibrosis along the left vagal trunk. Intraoperative tests showed severe bradycardia, but postoperatively this was not observed. Monitoring by Holter did not show any cardiac symptoms as the VNS parameters rose. The patient, who had initially responded to left-sided VNS with a 50 percent reduction in seizure frequency, returned to that same effectiveness level, though at a higher amplitude of stimulation.

Finally, two elderly patients obtained right-sided VNS in a separate case study, after surgical complications limited the use of left-sided VNS. Both patients endured uncomplicated surgical implantation on the right leg. Intraoperative lead checks showed no heart problems. Holter control was used in all cases on activation of the systems and on corresponding changes in amplitude. No cardiac side effects were observed in either case, and both reported a decrease of at least 50% in their rates of preoperative seizures.

Possible lateralization of the effects of vagus nerve stimulation In an interesting study, patients with left-sided VNS were examined with unexpected results.[12] All 47 patients surveyed received pre-operative examinations that included comprehensive psychiatric records, magnetic resonance imaging (MR) imaging, and long-term video telemetry that recorded images of ictal and interictal activities, allowing researchers to take part. Of those original 47 patients, 6 (13 percent) with left-sided VNS became completely seizure-free. Only one variable was independently correlated with complete seizure remission after reviewing all preoperative data to determine a predictive variable: lack of bilateral interictal epileptiform discharges. That is, left-sided VNS only produced seizure-free outcomes in patients who had interictal discharges lateralized. Remarkably, the authors, when asked about the laterality of the discharges, stated that five of the six patients who had become seizure-free from left-sided VNS had discharges situated to the left (ipsilateral) hemisphere (Janszky and Ebner, personal communication).

Such case cases offer important clues that may have been ignored for a long time because of early animal research studies. Stimulation of the right-sided cervical vagus nerve seems possible from both a safety and efficacy point of view. Second, to the ultimate goal of any epilepsy treatment, the laterality of VNS results may be important: full seizure remission. This laterality theory has yet to be routinely checked, but it is interesting to suggest that right-sided or even bilateral VNS in patients receiving sub-optimal results from left-sided VNS might be viable alternatives.

Conclusion

The special vagus nerve structure provides a convenient peripheral tool for affecting the brain without the intracranial surgery being invasive. Although clinical efficacy is often limited, VNS has been increasing, largely due to patient tolerance, protection, and low incidence of side effects. Future studies investigating the potential laterality of VNS effects, possibly leading to bilateral VNS, and further knowledge of fiber selectivity may contribute to therapeutic outcome changes not only for epilepsy but also for major depression and other future signs of VNS.

Chapter 5: Ways to unlock the power of the Vagus nerve

The vagus nerve is perhaps the essential nerve you didn't think you had.

Unlike other Vegas, there is no stay what happens in this vagus. The vagus nerve is a long meandering coil of motor and sensory fibers linking the brain stem to the heart, lungs, and intestines. It also branches out for the heart, spleen, gallbladder, ureter, female reproductive organs, arms, nose, tongue, and kidneys to touch and communicate. It stimulates our automatic nerve core— the parasympathetic nervous system— which regulates the unconscious functions of the body, as well as anything from rapid heart rate which absorption of food to respiration and sweating. This also helps maintain blood pressure and blood glucose levels, facilitates overall renal activity, helps release bile and hormones, encourages saliva production, helps suppress taste and remove tears, and plays a significant part in women's reproductive issues and orgasms.

Dr. Justin Hoffman, a certified naturopathic medical practitioner from Santa Rosa, California, says: Without the vagus nerve core functions that hold us alive would not be sustained.

Brandon Mentore, a nationally known sports nutritionist, strength and conditioning specialist, points out: The vagus nerve is highly vital to your physical wellbeing and is closely connected to numerous organs and body systems.

The vagus nerve has fibers that penetrate nearly all of our internal organs. Managing and managing emotions happens through the vagal nerve between the heart, brain, and stomach, which is why we respond intensely to extreme mental and emotional states.

5.1. How to hack your nervous system?

Vagus nerve dysfunction can lead to a whole host of issues, including hypertension, bradycardia (abnormally sluggish heartbeat), swallowing difficulty, gastrointestinal diseases, fainting, mood disturbances, B12 deficiency, systemic inflammation, irregular cough, and seizures. While the activation of the vagus nerve has been found to improve symptoms such as:

- Nervous disorder
- Lung attack
- Tinnitus
- Diabetes
- Drug abuse
- Migraines
- Alzheimer's
- Leaky stomach
- Poor breathing
- Anxiety disorder
- Cancer

A Closer Look at This Super Nerve

The most powerful of our 12 cranial nerves is the vagus nerve. Only the column of the spinal cord becomes a larger nervous system. Around 80% of the nerve fibers— or four of its five' lanes'—drive input to the brain from the body. The fifth lane travels in the reverse direction, blocking out brain impulses in the body. The vagus, rooted in the brain stem, passes across the spine and through the chest and splits between the left vagus and the right vagus. Each of these roads is comprised of hundreds of thousands of nerve fibers extending into the abdomen's heart, lungs, intestine, pancreas, and almost every other organ.

The neurotransmitter acetylcholine is used by the vagus nerve and activates muscle contractions in the parasympathetic nervous system. A neurotransmitter is a kind of chemical messenger produced at the end of a nerve fiber, facilitating the passage of impulses from point to point, activating various organs. Of starters, if our brain did not interact with our diaphragm by extracting acetylcholine from the nerve of the vagus, then we would stop breathing.

Many substances like botox and the heavy metal mercury can interfere with the production of acetylcholine. The vagus nerve, which induces death, was believed to be shut down by Botox. Mercury blocks the acetylcholine effect. As mercury binds to the thiol protein in the receptors of the cardiac muscle, the heart muscle is unable to receive electrical contraction impulse from the vagus nerve. Usually, the health complications follow. Mercury found just inches from the brain in fillings, as well as 3,000 tons of mercury released into the atmosphere, will compete with the development of acetylcholine. Mercury laden vaccines may also play a part in children with autism-linked to the vagus nerves. Hoffman says: Theoretically, something that helps to enhance acetylcholine's existence and function would also help to control the health of our vagus nerve.

To improve the sensitivity of acetylcholine receptors, he proposes natural nootropics huperzine and galantamine. Diabetes, smoking, upper respiratory bacterial infections, or having part of the nerve unintentionally cut during surgery can also cause vagus nerve injury. Heat, along with exhaustion and fear, can also inflame the nerve. Even the vagus nerve may be adversely affected by anything as basic as poor posture.

The effect of stress

Stress, along with exhaustion and anxiety, will inflame the vagus nerve.

It is also believed that food plays a part in the health of the vagus nerves. The vagus nerve's sensitivity is diminished by an obesogenic' cafeteria diet' (high- fat, high-carb fast food). Spicy foods will misfire, too.

A Pain in the Gut

According to Dr. Mark Sircus, acupuncturist, and professor of Oriental and biblical medicine, when people say they sense it in their intestines, that's not just imagination. The gut impulses are not delusions but true nervous signs that direct a large deal of the lives.

That is because the enteric nervous system (ENS), which regulates the gastrointestinal tract function, interacts through the vagus nerve to the central nervous system (the brain). That is known as the axis of the gut-brain. The ENS is often referred to as the second brain based on our solar plexus, or backup brain. Sircus continues: We also realize that the ENS is capable not only of control but also of controlling the brain. In addition, nearly 90 percent of the impulses that travel down the vagus nerve does not originate from above, but from the ENS. Maintaining the gut and vagus nerve gateway stable affects mental health. A new research showed how antibiotics, as they disrupt the microbial equilibrium in our body, can make us aggressive. Last year a major study by McMaster University in Hamilton, Ontario, Canada, showed that certain helpful gut microbes could potentially prevent PTSD. According to a study in the National Center for Biotechnology Knowledge (NCBI), probiotics will help maintain the gut and vagus nerve signals in a safer state.

Mental wellbeing and the vagus nerve.

Keeping the nerve path to the stomach and vagus stable affects our emotional health.

Dr. Abby Kramer, a holistic healer, and chiropractor in Glenview, Illinois, explains: Because of its relation to the stomach and intestinal processes, probiotics help encourage vagal activity. Zinc is also a perfect help to those with depression or mental health issues, and it also ties up with the vagus nerve.

Boosting With Electricity

Doctors have abused the power of the nerve upon the brain for a long time. Electrical vagus nerve stimulation, or vagus nerve stimulation (VNS), is often used in treating patients with epilepsy or depression. VNS is intended to avoid seizures by sending normal, mild bursts of electrical energy from the vagus nerve to the brain. Such pulses receive something like a pacemaker from a system. This is mounted on the chest wall under the muscle, and a cable extends from it to the neck's vagus nerve. Researchers researching the impact of vagus stimulation on epilepsy found that a second advantage due to seizure control was felt by patients: their moods have changed.

A 2016 research published in the National Academy of Sciences (PNAS) Proceedings revealed how to activate the vagus nerve using a bioelectronic system, a chronic inflammatory condition that affects 1.3 million people in the United States and costs tens of billions of dollars annually to treat.

5.2. 12 vagus nerve stimulation techniques

No need to shake the vagus nerve into form. Similar to a muscle, it can also be toned and reinforced. Below are a few easy things you can do that will significantly boost your health:

1. Optimistic Social Relationships–People in a survey needed to think compassionately of others while silently sharing positive thoughts of friends and families. The meditators displayed an average improvement in optimistic feelings such as serenity, happiness, and hope after the

lesson was finished compared with the controllers. Such optimistic feelings from others lead to an increase in vagal activity, as seen in the variation of the heart rate. The tests have shown a more toned vagus nerve than when meditating literally.

2. Cold-"The cold treatment such as ice baths or face dunking often activates the nerve," Mentore says.

Studies suggest that the fight or flight (sympathetic) response reduces as the body responds to cold, while the rest while eating (parasympathetic) response increases -and this is regulated by the vagus nerve. Any form of acute cold exposure like drinking ice cold water may increase the stimulation of the vagus nerves.

3. Gargling-Gargling of water is another home cure for an under-stimulated vagus nerve. Gargling activates the pallet muscles where the vagus nerve is shot to.

"Usually, people are going to tear up a little, which is a positive indication because if they don't, we suggest that they do so on a daily basis every day before they find they are tearing up a little," Hoffman says. "It was found to enhance the efficiency of working memory straight away."

4. Singing And Repeating-Humming, chanting a prayer, singing hymns, and cheerful, enthusiastic singing all increase heart rate variability (HRV) in slightly different ways. Singing is basically like activating a vagal pump, which sends out calming waves. Singing at the top of your lungs works to activate the vagus by muscles in the back of the throat. Singing in unison, often done in churches and synagogues, increases the function of HRV and vagus, too. It was discovered that singing increases oxytocin, also

known as the love hormone, because it makes people feel attached to each other. Compassion Meditation has been shown to produce a more toned nerve of the vagus.

5. Massage-You can stimulate your vagus nerve by massaging your feet and neck along the carotid sinus on either side of your neck, located along the carotid arteries. A neck massage can help to decrease seizures. A foot massage help can reduce your blood pressure and heart rate. A massage with pressure can also activate the vagus nerve. These massages are used to help infants gain weight by stimulating gut function, which is largely mediated by vagus nervous activation.

6. Laughter–Feeling happy and laughing are normal immune boosters. Also, the vagus nerve is stimulated by Laughter. The research shows how laughter in a group environment increases HRV.

There are numerous case reports of laughter-fainting individuals, and this may be due to too much activation of the vagus nerve / parasympathetic system. Fainting will occur after laughing as well as urination, nausea, vomiting or bowel movement — all aided by stimulation of the vagus.

7. Yoga and Tai Chi — All improve vagus nerve function and therefore improve the parasympathetic system. Studies have shown that yoga raises GABA, a neurotransmitter that calms the brain. Scientists assume this is achieved by "stimulating vagal afferents (fibers)," which enhance parasympathetic nervous system function. It is of special support to those who deal with anxiety or depression.

Studies show that tai chi can also' better vagal synchronization '

8. Breathing Deeply and Slowly – The nerves in your heart and neck have receptors called baroreceptors that sense blood pressure and relay the neuronal signal to your brain. It stimulates the heart-connecting vagus nerve to lower blood pressure and heart rate. Slow ventilation, with roughly the same amount of time breathing in and out, increases baroreceptor sensitivity and vagal response. In the average adult, it can be very beneficial to breathe about 5-6 breaths per minute.

9. Activity-Exercise increases the growth hormone in your brain, strengthens mitochondria in your liver, and helps to prevent cognitive decline. Yet stimulating the vagus nerve has also been shown which contributes to beneficial effects on the brain and mental health. In fact, light activity increases bowel blood, which is regulated by the vagus nerve.

In a group environment, Laughter is a normal immune boosterLaughter activates the vagus nerve and raises HRV.

10. Coffee Enemas– Enemas to the vagus nerve are like sprints. Expanding the bowel, as is achieved in enemas, increases the activation of the vagus nerve. This removal is achieved by increasing the capacity of the liver to detoxify toxins in the blood and attach them to the bile. The liver cleans itself in the process as it removes the poisonous bile for evacuation into the small, then large, intestine. Every three minutes, the whole bloodstream circulates through the liver. The blood can flow four or five times for washing by keeping the caffeine for 12 or 15 minutes, just like a

dialysis procedure. The coffee's water content induces intestinal peristalsis and helps with the stored poisonous bile drain the large intestine.

11. Nervana – This wearable device sends a soft electrical pulse through the left ear canal to activate the vagus nerve of the body while synchronizing with music, which in effect, activates the release of neurotransmitters throughout the brain that produce a soothing feeling in the body.

12. Relax–Learning how to relax could be the No. 1 thing that helps to keep the vagus tense. Most calming practices, Hoffman states, should improve the vagus nerve.

In the end, this is where the most profoundly felt impacts can be made. Reading a book, listening to music, watching kids play–whatever it may be, my advice is to try pleasure and make time for that in your life. Dr. Jan Hoffman.

Kevin Tracey, a New York-based neurosurgeon, is a man plagued by personal events-a task man. "My mother died when I was five years old from a brain tumor. This was really unexpected, and shocking, "he says. "So from that perspective, I knew that the brain-nerves-were important for wellbeing." This history makes him a neurosurgeon who knows a lot about inflammation. He claims it was this insight that helped him to view a new way of understanding the effects of an accidental experiment.

Stimulating Results Tracey developed the experiment with his partner, Paul- Peter Tak, University of Amsterdam professor of rheumatology. Tak has long found an alternative to powerful medications that would inhibit the immune response for treating rheumatoid arthritis.

"Immune reaction from the body only is a problem when it affects your own body rather than foreign cells, or when it becomes chronic," he concluded. "Then the problem becomes: How do we strengthen the process of shutting off the body?"When Tracey called him to say that the solution could be to activate the vagus nerve by turning off TNF output, Tak immediately saw the opportunity and was excited to see how it might succeed. Vagal nerve stimulation has already been licensed for epilepsy in humans, and it would be fairly easy to gain permission for an arthritis trial.

And the participants had positive interactions at the trial. The findings are still being prepared for review, but Tak claims more than half of the patients demonstrated considerable progress, and almost one-third are in remission–in turn, healed of their rheumatoid arthritis. Not only did seventeen of the 20 participants in the study feel better, but swelling levels in their blood also went down. Others are now drug-free entirely.

"We've seen really strong patterns of three-minute relaxation a day," says Tak.

Tak believes patients will also require life-stimulation of the vagal nerves. Yet compared to the drugs that work by blocking the development of immune cells and proteins like TNF, vagal nerve stimulation tends to maintain the natural balance of the body. This decreases over-production of TNF, which causes chronic inflammation but does not impair proper immune function, so the body can respond to infection in a normal way.

Changing the Tone A dangerous treatment is to have an electronic device surgically inserted into your body for the remainder of your career. Yet the procedure has been so effective–and so attractive to doctors–that other experts are now looking into using vagal nerve stimulation for a number of other chronic painful disorders, including inflammatory bowel disease, asthma, diabetes, chronic fatigue syndrome, and obesity.

There are tremendous benefits of being able to boost the vagal sound easily and efficiently, and thereby reduce significant public health challenges such as medical diseases and diabetes. It has the power to alter entirely the way we view disease. Unless the doctor's appointment included monitoring the vagal tone as quickly as, for example, we measure blood pressure; treatments might be administered to boost it. Yet that's also a long way off: "We don't even know what a safe vagal sound sounds like yet," researcher Bethany Kok cautions.

What is more likely in the near term is that implants will be inserted with certain disorders that are actually being treated by drugs: "When technology advances and these instruments get smaller and more reliable," says Kevin Tracey, "I envisage a day when neural circuit control systems with bioelectronic medicine will be injected–they will either be put under local anesthesia or under mild sedation. "It's becoming abundantly clear that we can't see organs in isolation as we did in the past," Paul-Peter Tak says. "It seems obvious, but that's not how we looked at it before." This article originally appeared on Mosaic and has been republished in a revised version here.

Top illustration by CWA Studios / Shutterstock obesity neuroscience Tracey dealt with a rat's head in the late 1990s. "We must have inserted an anti- inflammatory drug into the brain, and after a stroke, we examined the positive effect of suppressing inflammation," he says. "We were shocked to find that it also suppressed inflammation of spleen and other organs in the rest of the body, while the drug was present in the brain. But the amount of medication we had ingested was much too small to reach into the bloodstream and spread to the rest of the body. "After months of thinking over this, he eventually came up with the notion that the brain could use the nervous system–the vagus nerve in particular–to instruct the spleen to stop inflammation anywhere.

It was an amazing concept-if Tracey. It was correct, and the brain was actively controlling the inflammation of body tissues. Communication between the expert cells of the immune system in our lungs and bloodstream and the nervous system's electrical connections has been thought unlikely. So Tracey clearly noticed that the two structures were intricately intertwined.

Cutting the vagus nerve was the first crucial examination of the promising theory. When Tracey and his colleagues did, the infusion of the anti- inflammatory drug into the brain had little effect on the rest of the body any more. The second study was for activating the nerve in the body without any drug. "Since the vagus nerve, like all nerves, channels information through electrical impulses, this meant we would be able to duplicate the procedure through inserting a nerve stimulator on the vagus nerve in the brainstem to suppress the spleen inflammation," he says. "The Wandering Nerve ' Vagus' is Latin for' walking' and indeed this bundle of nerve fibers rotates through the body, networking the brain with the stomach and digestive tract, the lungs, heart, spleen, intestines, liver and kidneys, not to mention a range of other nerves involved in speech, eye contact, facial expressions... This is made up of thousands and thousands of fibers, and 80% of them are visual, which ensures that the vagus nerve sends back to the brain what is happening in your organs.

Nevertheless, not all vagus nerves are the same: some people have more vagus activity, which means that their bodies can relax more easily after a pain. The frequency of the vagus reaction is known as the vagal pulse, and heart rate can be calculated with an electrocardiogram. Your heart beats harder every time you breathe in, to accelerate the flow of oxygenated blood through the body. Breathe slowly and slow the heart rate. This variation is one of the factors that the vagus nerve controls and is activated when you breathe out but inhibited when you breathe in, and the greater the heart rate difference as you breathe in and out, the stronger the vagal tone would be.

Study indicates that a high vagal tone increases the body's capacity to control blood glucose rates, raising the risk of diabetes, stroke, and cardiovascular diseases. However, the weak vagal tone was related to systemic inflammation. Inflammation plays a valuable function as part of the immune system to help the body heal following an injury, for example, but it will destroy organs and blood vessels if it continues when it is not required.

Having found evidence of a role for the vagus in a number of chronic inflammatory disorders like rheumatoid arthritis,

Tracey and his colleagues tried to see if it could turn into a possible treatment pathway. The vagus nerve acts as a conduit that carries electrochemical signals between the organs and the brain. Tracey found that signals from the brain asking the spleen to shut down the development of a specific inflammatory protein, tumor necrosis factor (TNF), had not been received in chronic inflammatory disease. Maybe they could raise the signals?

5.3. Vagus nerve is key to well-being

Have you ever read something up to one day a million times, for no particular cause, say, "Wait, what is that?" This happened to me the other day because of' the vagus nerve.' I kept running across it in relation to deep breathing and mental calmness:' Breathing deeply,' writes Katie Brindle in her latest book Yang Sheng: The Art of Chinese Self-Healing,' relaxes the body instantly because it activates the vagus nerve which runs from the neck to the abdomen and is responsible for shutting off the' fight or flight.'

I loved this notion that under our skin, we have something like a hidden piano key to click internally to calm us down. And as if to pluck a musical line. I pictured the vagus nerve as a single inner cord at this level, extending from the head to the stomach. In addition, the vagus nerve is a squiggly, shaggy, branching nerve that links most of the main organs between the brain and colon, like a root or cable chain. This is the longest nerve of the body, and it comes functionally with a combination of two vagus nerves, one for the body's right and one for the left. It is called "vagus" because it wanders around the bodies, like a vagabond. The vagus nerve was described as "widely responsible for the link between the mind and the body," for its function as a mediator between thinking and emotion, and I am inclined to think of it as more of a physical embodiment of the soul. Also: "As people say' trust your heart,'" as one of Psychology Today's authors put it many years earlier, "they actually mean' trust your vagus nerve.'" I was profoundly fascinated by that nerve, just though it seemed like I knew it less and less. How does all of that work? Why does a nerve trigger calms them down? Is this why I get angry over stuff so needlessly?

"Stimulating the heart's vagus nerve has a very strong effect on reducing the heart rate," said NYU-Langone associate professor of neurology Lucy Norcliffe-Kaufmann. So that, in fact, is what helps them comfortably. The vagus nerve actually responds to the way we breathe, which delivers whatever message our breath suggests to the brain and the heart. For e.g., breathing reduces the oxygen demands of the cardiac muscle (myocardium), and our heart rate decreases.

The vagus nerve is actually the queen of the parasympathetic nervous system — known as the "rest and sleep" or the "chill out" one — and the more we do things that "stimulate" or trigger it, such as deep breathing, the more we banish the effects of the sympathetic nervous system— known as the "fight or turn" organ. "Adrenaline / cortisol-releasing pain'.

Put another way: "The body feels the breathing and in turn adapts its heart rate," Norcliffe-Kaufmann told me. When we breathe in, she explained, the sensory nodes in our lungs ("lung stretch receptors") transmit information through the vagus nerve and through the brain, and when we breathe out, the brain sends information back down through the vagus nerve to delay or stimulate the heart. So the heart speeds down as we breathe steadily, and we relax. By comparison, our heart speeds up as we breathe rapidly, and we feel amputated or nervous.

I was shocked by the fact that it is the exhale that activates the relief reaction, but Norcliffe-Kaufmann confirmed: "Vagal movement is the highest and the lowest heart rate when you exhale." She said that the perfect, most relaxing way to breathe is six times a minute: five seconds in, five seconds out. She also noted that researchers found in the analysis that calculated this pace that this type of slow breathing is often what practitioners usually fall into with mantras during meditation, and with rosaries during the Ave Maria prayer. "Every time you do either a rosary or a meditation chant," said Norcliffe- Kaufmann, "it automatically synchronizes your breathing at six times a minute." ("It's interesting," I said. "It's!" she said.) It made me wonder whether there are ways to quantify the consistency of the vagus nerve, or "vagal sound," as defined by Norcliffe-Kaufmann. Basically, this is how safe, strong, and functional the nerve is. One approach, she said, is to calculate the difference of heart rate (HRV) — it's a kind of "surrogate" for measuring real vagal tone (open chest surgery). Variability of heart rhythm is the degree the heart rate fluctuates between a breath in (when it spontaneously accelerates) and a breath out (when it naturally slows down). That is, on inhalation, heart rate increases and falls on exhalation, and the disparity between those two rates effectively tests vagal tone. For starters, athletes are known to have higher vagal tone while individuals who undergo prolonged stretches of bed rest— and astronauts in conditions with no-gravity — are known to have lower vagal tone. (How fast the heart rate slows after exercise is also a strong vagal tone marker.) Vagus nerve stimulation has also been suggested as a means to combat alcohol (some heavy drinkers have poor vagal tone, for example).

Certain devices measure HRV — and I've personally tried a chest strap and a wristband, but I got stumped on what to do with the data— although Norcliffe-Kaufmann is skeptical about their reliability. "These developments are arriving," she said, "but it's more important to concentrate on breathing and to keep relaxed and healthy than on a figure." Several other techniques believed to boost the vagal tone (beyond gentle, steady breathing) involve smiling, singing, chanting, meditation, acupuncture, and splashing the face with cold water— or doing a full-body cold rinse. (Stimulation of the vagus nerve, both manually and with electricity, was also used to regulate hallucinations in patients with epilepsy, to alleviate anxiety, and to relieve psychiatric depression.) Writing this story, I found myself breathing more slowly and feeling calmer after interacting with Norcliffe-Kaufmann. Not really pleased, but stubborn. Slow breathing is dull but how successful it is almost sad. I will normally prefer to spend hundreds of dollars on getting a tracker to control myself, rather than doing this free and more successful thing.

"If you're in a tense situation," said Norcliffe-Kaufmann, "and you're like, how do I respond? When you intentionally slow down your breathing for only one minute or just a few seconds, you will put yourself in a calmer state to communicate better.

Chapter 6: Healing Power of Vagus nerve against Inflammation

Inflammation is a system for protection within the body. The immune system detects weakened cells, irritants, and infections, and it continues the process of healing.

If a part of our body is disturbed by something unpleasant or irritating, there is a biochemical reaction to seek to eliminate it. The inflammatory signs and symptoms may be painful, but they are a reminder that the body is attempting to repair itself.

6.1. What is Inflammation?

Inflammation is a part of the immune response from the body. For example, when the knee sustains an impact, it may be helpful, and tissues need care and protection. Nevertheless, inflammation can sometimes continue longer than necessary, causing more harm than good.

Inflammatory effects differ according to whether the response is acute or chronic.

The PRISH acronym will sum up the effects of acute inflammation. They include Pain: The area that is inflamed is likely to be painful, particularly during and after contact. Chemicals are released, which stimulate nerve endings and make the area more receptive.

Redness: This is because the underlying capillaries are filled with blood more than normal.

Immobility: The region of inflammation can cause any loss of function.

Swelling: An accumulation of fluid triggers this.

Heat: More blood flows to the affected area, and that makes contact feel warm.

Those five acute symptoms of inflammation refer only to skin inflammations. If inflammation happens deep within the body, for example, in an internal organ, only some of the symptoms may be visible. For example, certain internal organs may not have adjacent sensory nerve endings, so there will be no discomfort, as in some forms of inflammation of the lungs.

Chronic inflammatory symptoms occur in a different way, which can include: nausea mouth sores stomach pain fever rash joint pain. A person may experience signs of inflammation after these measures.

6.2. Causes of inflammation

Inflammation is caused by a variety of physical responses induced in response to a physical injury or an illness by the immune system.

Inflammation doesn't automatically mean an infection is present, but an infection may induce inflammation.

Three major mechanisms occur before and after acute inflammation: when delivering blood to the affected area, the small branches of the arteries widen, contributing to decreased blood flow. Capillaries are safer for the penetration of fluids and molecules, which ensures they can travel between the cells and blood.

Acute inflammation is one that begins quickly and gets serious in a short time. Signs and symptoms are usually apparent only for a few days, but, in some cases, can last for a few weeks.

Types of illnesses, disorders, and circumstances that can contribute to severe inflammation include:

- severe bronchitis
- contaminated toenail
- a sore throat from a cold or flu
- acute appendicitis
- tonsillitis
- infective sinusitis
- a physical wound

6.3. Chronic or acute inflammation

These are the two forms of inflammation, depending on how much the symptoms intensify and how long they last.

The table below illustrates the important distinctions between acute and chronic inflammation:

	Acute	Chronic
Caused by	Harmful bacteria or tissue injury	Pathogens that the body cannot break down, including some types of virus, foreign bodies that remain in the system, or overactive immune responses
Onset	Rapid	Slow
Duration	A few days	From months to years
Outcomes	Inflammation improves, turns into an abscess, or becomes chronic	Tissue death and the thickening and scarring of connective tissue

Chronic Inflammation

It leads to inflammation in the long term, which will last for several months or years. It can result from failure to remove something that triggered an acute infection, an autoimmune condition that affects normal healthy tissue, mistaking it for a pathogen that triggers exposure to the disease at a low level of a single irritant, such as industrial chemicals, for a long period of time. It is important to control the inflammation well. It also hurts because you get inflammation.

Depending on the extent of the infection, people can experience pressure, swelling, nausea, anxiety, and even suffering, specific forms of discomfort. It may be defined as slow, continuous, throbbing, pulsating, punching, or pinching. Inflammation causes inflammation mainly as the swelling presses against the delicate nerve endings. That gives out messages of distress to the brain.

During inflammation, other biochemical processes occur too. We affect how the muscles function, and that can cause discomfort.

6.4. Common Treatments

Inflammation, as stated earlier in this chapter, is part of the healing cycle. Reducing inflammation is often beneficial but not always necessary.

Anti-inflammatory medicines

It is possible to take non-steroidal anti-inflammatory drugs (NSAIDs) to alleviate the discomfort caused by inflammation. They function against an enzyme that contributes to inflammation. It avoids discomfort or growing it.

Definitions of NSAIDs include naproxen, ibuprofen, and aspirin, available for on-line purchase. Evite long-term use of NSAIDs until a doctor recommends They raise the risk of a person developing stomach ulcers, which can lead to serious, life-threatening bleeding. NSAIDs can also aggravate symptoms of asthma, cause kidney damage, and increase the risk of stroke or heart attacks.

Acetaminophen can relieve discomfort without causing the swelling, such as paracetamol or Tylenol. They could be suitable for those who only want to relieve the pain while encouraging the inflammation's healing factor to continue.

Corticosteroids

Corticosteroids, such as cortisol, are a class of steroid hormones that prevent a variety of inflammatory mechanisms. There are two types of corticosteroids:

Glucocorticoids: these are used for a variety of conditions, including arthritis temporal arteritis dermatitis inflammatory bowel disease (IBS) systemic lupus hepatitis asthma allergic reactions sarcoidosis creams and ointments may be recommended for ears, hair, kidneys, intestines and nasal inflammations.

Mineralocorticoids: For people with adrenal insufficiency, they are used to treat cerebral salt loss and to remove essential hormones. If ingested by mouth, the side-effects of corticosteroids are more probable. Taking inhalers or injections with them will reduce the risk.

Inhaled medications, such as those used to treat asthma in the long term, raise the risk of contracting oral thrush. After might use, mouth rinsing out with water can help prevent oral thrush.

Glucocorticoids can also cause Cushing's disease, while mineralocorticoids can cause elevated blood pressure, low blood potassium levels, weakening in the connective tissue, and complications with body tissue levels in acids and alkalis.

6.5. Reducing inflammation starts with Vagus nerve

The underlying cause of most chronic illnesses is inflammation, and the vagus nerve plays a vital function in reducing inflammation. Master the natural abdominal massage technique to stimulate this nerve and help regulate your immune system, relax your mind and body, and reduce inflammation.

Inflammation is the underlying cause of most serious diseases. Although acute inflammation can be helpful as a part of the immune and healing processes, as it is chronic or unbalanced, inflammation may affect the body. Chronic, systemic, and low-grade inflammation is a significant contributor to aging, asthma, and chronic disorders such as Alzheimer's Type 2 Diabetes, Atherosclerosis, Arthritis, Connection between Anxiety, Inflammation, and Immune System. The vagus nerve (cranial nerve X) is the primary nerve of the autonomous nervous system's parasympathetic (rest and digest) portion. This is an essential contact path between the brain, cardiovascular system, intestines, and immune system. This bi-directional nerve system passes across the chest and through the abdomen all the way from the brainstem, and branches out through several organs. This wide route gave birth to its name, vagus, which means "rolling" in Latin

The body is closely interrelated, and the vagus nerve plays a significant part in organizing contacts. Signals are conveyed from the brain to chest and abdominal tissues, as well as back to the central nervous system from the stomach and liver. Through signaling the brain to produce neurotransmitters and hormones, organizing responses, controlling stress reactions, and helping to keep inflammation in check, the vagus nerve helps orchestrate this coordination network.

For example, the vagus nerve plays a key role in organizing the response to parasympathetic relief, helping to slow down breathing and heart rate, encouraging sleep, enhancing digestion, and fostering a feeling of peace and quiet. The vagus nerve produces the neurotransmitter acetylcholine, which tends to be a significant brake on inflammation in the body, to better guide the relaxing response.

Since the vagal nerve is a major control center for the body, the health of this nerve is of vital importance for the health of the brain, immune system, and overall inflammatory condition. Some individuals have more nerve vagus function than others, which helps their bodies to relax quicker after pain. The intensity of the reaction to the vagus is known as vagal sound.

Chronic inflammation has been linked with the weak vagal register. Evidencc suggests that people with inflammatory disorders such as rheumatoid arthritis and other autoimmune diseases have frequently diminished variation of heart rate, which is a sign of reduced vagal sound. This decreased vagal tone stimulates the development of pro-inflammatory cytokines (substances secreted by inflammatory cells and influencing other cells), which contributes to an increase in sympathetic nervous system function, which stress hormones, leading to systemic inflammation.

Abdominal massage is a Natural Anti-Inflammatory method

Luckily, by using natural methods, you can stimulate this nerve and improve your vagal tone to better regulate the immune system, relax the body and mind, and reduce inflammation. Work indicates that stimulating the vagus nerve serves as a natural anti-inflammatory and relaxing agent as it decreases pro-inflammatory cytokine production and calms the nervous system.

A type of self-abdominal massage is an evolving technique for minimizing inflammation and toning the vagus nerve. Strong pressure stimulation has been found to activate the vagus nerve, enhance the flow and output of the digestive tract, and boost the production of insulin to better regulate blood sugar in preterm babies (adult trials are yet to be done). The combination of manual manipulation and vagus nerve stimulation can have potent anti- inflammatory benefits.

How to do Abdominal Massage

In just a few minutes, this abdominal massage procedure is simple to do at home. This procedure is better done on an empty stomach, a couple of hours after feeding. Start slowly to see how the body reacts. Lie on a soft floor mat or on a bunk.

Place your hand beneath your breastbone or sternum. Allow soft, stroking downward movements – moving your hand down into your belly. Perform this action for a few minutes, riding in a backward bike-pedaling–like gesture, one side over the other.

Next, make tiny circular movements on your abdomen with your fingertips. Start massaging your abdomen's sides and work your way slowly inwards and downwards. Go deeper slowly, using a solid and relaxed amount of pressure. Keep on for several minutes of this abdominal massage. Then finish the session with a relaxed reclined two-knee spinal twist pose (Supta Matsyendrasana) for a few minutes. This restorative pose of yoga promotes digestion and facilitates an opening in the fascia and diaphragm to help intensify the breath and promote an anti-inflammatory reaction to relaxation.

Lying on your stomach, exhale as you gently press your butt back onto the floor or bed. Breathe in here for a few moments while you open your lower back. When primed, contract your abdominal muscles softly as you inhale and bend your knees towards your shoulders. Exhale with your hands against the surface, also with your back, and push your arms out to your side.

Lift your feet somewhat higher than your knees on a gradual inhalation, then slowly drop both legs to the left toward the floor while you exhale. Hold your thighs close up to the point of your shoulders and your feet and elbows. Rest 30-60 seconds in this pose. Continue to take long, deep breaths as you slowly move from side to side, with your breath going. Try the easy exercise to reach your vagus nerve's capacity. Perform these methods for several weeks for a few minutes, once or twice a day. The rewards of reduced stress, improved digestion, better detoxification, decreased pain, and squelched inflammation can surprise you!

6.6. The anti-inflammatory effect of vagal stimulation

Throughout the sense of inflammation by different molecular mechanisms, the principal autonomic neurotransmitters, acetylcholine, and noradrenaline, are implicated throughout immune control. Circadian oscillations in autonomic nervous system activity allow for concerted immune cell response.

Recent experiments have not only established the correlation between the nervous system and the immune system. We explained that one well- characterized cytokine-inhibiting system, called the "inflammatory reflex," is based on nerve impulses from the vagus. A neural circuit that controls the immune response to injury and invasion activates this inflammatory reflex. The Reflex afferent arc is stimulated by cytokines and is transferred to ambiguous medullary nucleus sympathoexcitatory neurons. The efferent vagal arc actively suppresses the production of cytokines and thereby reduces inflammation and prevents organ damage. Experimental data obtained in rats suggest that cytokine production may be inhibited and arthritis attenuated by vagal stimulation (Levine YA et al. Cholinergic anti-inflammatory pathway neurostimulation improves disease in collagen-induced arthritis in rats.

Kilohertz nerve block frequency enhances the anti-inflammatory effects of stimulation of the vagus nerves. Scientific Reports, Combining a 60s cervical vagus nerve stimulation (cVNS) of 10-Hz, once daily with kilohertz nerve block of afferent vagal nerve fibers, Yogi Patel et al. from the Department of Biomedical Engineering, Georgia

Institute of Technology was able to selectively improve vagus nerve efference and inhibit the peripheral production of TNF, IL-1β andIL-6. Selective activation of the efferent cVNS has anti-inflammatory effects. Their findings also found that this anti- inflammatory effect is strengthened by the entire afferent nervous system.

The activation of the nerve vagus reduces cytokine output and attenuates the frequency of inflammation in rheumatoid arthritis. In their carefully documented study of patients undergoing stimulation of the vagus nerve to decrease the occurrence of epileptic seizures, Koopman et al. found that the stimulation of the vagus nerve (up to four times daily) has had an effect on rheumatoid arthritis disease. The activation of the vagus nerve greatly impaired the development of TNF by up to 84 d. In fact, the seriousness of the disorder, as calculated by standardized scientific composite ratings, significantly increased. Together these findings indicate that activation of the vagus nerve modulates the development of TNF and decreases inflammation in humans. An increasing number of vagus nerve-focused neuromodulation trials lead to a new, non-pharmacological approach to support rheumatoid arthritis treatment and probably other autoimmune and autoinflammatory diseases.

Chapter 7: Vagus Nerve and Neuro-immune axis

The vagus nerve (VN) is the organism's longest nerve and a significant part of the parasympathetic nervous system, alongside the sympathetic nervous system, which forms the autonomic nervous system (ANS). Classically there is a balance between the sympathetic and parasympathetic nervous systems that are responsible for preserving homeostasis. Under different pathologic circumstances, an Ants mismatch is observed. A hybrid nerve with 4/5 afferent and 1/5 efferent fibers, the VN is a central component of the neuroimmune and brain-gut axes via bidirectional coordination between the brain and the gastrointestinal (GI) tract. A dual anti-inflammatory function of the VN is identified using either vagal afferents that target the hypothalamic- pituitary-adrenal axis or vagal efferents that target the anti-inflammatory cholinergic pathway. The sympathetic nervous system and the VN work in combination to prevent the release of tumor necrosis factor-alpha (TNFα) by peripheral tissue and spleen macrophages via the splenic nerve. The VN is a clinical target in the treatment of chronic inflammatory diseases, where TNFα is a central component because of its anti-inflammatory effect. In this study, the emphasis will be on the VN's anti-inflammatory role in inflammatory bowel disease (IBD). The VN's anti-inflammatory effects may be activated by pharmacology, enteral diet, VN stimulation (VNS), complementary medicines, or physical activity. VNS is one of the experimental therapies for drug-resistant epilepsy and depression, and one would imagine that VNS might be used as a non-drug therapy to combat inflammatory GI tract conditions such as IBD, irritable bowel syndrome, and postoperative ileus, both of which are characterized by a blunted autonomic equilibrium with decreased vagal tone.

7.1. Introduction

The vagus nerve (VN), the organism's longest nerve, makes the connection between the central nervous system and the body by inserting vital, visceral organs such as the heart, lungs, and gastrointestinal (GI) tract. The VN is a mixed nerve with twenty percent efferent and 80 percent afferent fibers, and a significant part of the parasympathetic nervous system that makes up the autonomic nervous system (ANS) alongside the sympathetic nervous system. The sympathetic and parasympathetic nervous systems for preserving homeostasis are classically regulated. In different pathologies such as irritable bowel syndrome (IBS), inflammatory bowel disorders (IBD), rheumatoid arthritis (RA), and others, this equilibrium of the ANS is impaired, and such an imbalance may also be an indicator of multiple neuroimmune disorder. In fact, the progression of chronic inflammatory disorders such as RA is accompanied by autonomic dysfunction, as illustrated by poor parasympathetic involvement. Autonomic dysfunction may also be implicated in the etiopathogenesis of inflammatory disorders rather than being the product of pathological inflammation. ANS control, in particular by manipulating the VN, is capable of enhancing various neurological conditions such as inflammatory disorders, including IBD, RA, obesity, and pain. These control of the VN is possible by pharmacological induction, VN stimulation (VNS), dietary therapy, physical activity, and complementary medications. Classically, the VN does not innervate lymphoid organs; the sympathetic nervous system is devoted to that function. Neuro-immune system, however, includes the VN both by its afferent and efferent fibers. Indeed, the VN activates the axis of hypothalamic–pituitary–adrenal (HPA) to produce glucocorticoids through the adrenal glands via its afferent fibers. The VN also participates in the cholinergic anti-inflammatory pathway (CAP) by a vago-vagal reflex that requires an interconnected brainstem contact between vagal afferent and efferent fibers, i.e., the inflammatory reflex. The sympathetic nervous system and the VN communicate via both a vago-sympathetic pathway involving vagal afferent fibers and a vago-splenic pathway through vagal efferent fibers. Consequently, the VN is at the crossroads of neuro-immune reactions, and various inflammatory diseases of the organism may be controlled by stimulating the VN.

In the present paper, we will first define the anatomy of the VN, second, identify the VN's associations with the HPA axis and the CAP and the sympathetic nervous system, third, discuss the importance of VN's therapeutic modulation for anti-inflammatory properties by pharmacological stimulation, VNS, complementary medicines (acupuncture, hypnosis, mindfulness), enteral nu

The VN internalizes all of the rat's GI tract, except the rectum. In comparison, the VN's innervation of the GI tract is discussed in humans. For certain writers, the VN innervates the digestive tract before the colon's splenic flexure, and the sacral parasympathetic nucleus innerves the remainder of the intestine via the pelvic nerves; the stomach is equipped with the densest innervation. The VN could, however, innervate all of the human digestive tract. The VN consists of 80% afferent fibers conveying flavor, visceral and somatic information, and 20% efferent fibers implicated in GI motility regulation and secretion, as well as cardiac parasympathetic sound and CAP.

Preganglionic vagal efferent neurons reside in the vagus ' dorsal motor nucleus (DMNV), below the nucleus tractus solitarius (NTS), where vagal afferents are projected to. In the rat DMNV, a viscerotropic distribution has been identified, so that lateral neurons innervate the stomach while the colon is innervated by the medial neurons. Preganglionic neurons in the GI tract are connected to enteric nervous system post-ganglionic neurons. Acetylcholine (ACh) is the neuromodulator released at both ends of these pre-and post- ganglionic neurons, binding respectively to nicotinic receptors and nicotinic or muscarinic receptors. The VN is not in direct communication with the intestinal lamina propria but through these enteric neurons, which are the VN's effectors for the control of intestinal immunity.

Vagal afferent fibers emerge from their cell bodies in the nodose ganglia, from the various intestinal layers. According to a rostrocaudal viscerotropic representation, they end in the NTS, and then to the postrema field. With the NTS and region postrema, the DMNV incorporates the brainstem's dorsal vagal center, a major ANS reflex center. Indeed, vagal afferent stimulation induces multiple co-ordinated responses (autonomic, endocrine, and behavioral) through core mechanisms, including the dorsal vagal complex. At the root of vago-vagal reflexes, viscerosensory information from the NTS to the DMNV affects vagal afferents. In addition, the NTS is a conduit for such peripheral knowledge to enter various brain regions forming the core autonomous network (CAN), such as the locus coeruleus (LC), the parabrachial (PB) nucleus, the pericentric nucleus of the thalamus, the core nucleus of the amygdala, the hypothalamus paraventricular nucleus (PVH), the medial preoptic lobe, the arcuate nucleus of the hypothalamus. The NTS modulates the LC and its predictions explicitly, too. The rostroventrolateral medulla is one of two major examples of LC predictions. In addition, the PB nucleus extends into the main nucleus of the amygdala, the stria terminalis bed nucleus, and the PVH. The PVH specifically designs with the NTS, thereby forming a feedback loop with the forebrain. Consequently, VN- driven visceral input (e.g., nutrient sensing) is introduced into the CAN involved in the processing of the ANS and the reaction to the HPA axis. The VN is interested in interoceptive perception, where the cortex of the insula plays a central role. A perturbation of this surveillance in digestive tract diseases such as IBS but even IBD is found. For both cases, alexithymia is clearly found.

7.2. The vagus nerve and neuro-immune axis

The VN, both by its afferent and efferent fibers, is a central component of the neuroimmune axis. Harris had first identified the role of vagal afferents in controlling the HPA axis. Indeed, peripheral lipopolysaccharide (LPS) administration, classically used as an experimental septic shock model, causes the activation of interleukin (IL)-1β, a pro-inflammatory cytokine, and eventually stimulates vagal afferents via IL-1 receptors. Vagotomy avoids this effect, and it acts in a dose-and receptor-dependent manner. Vagal afferents activate noradrenergic group A2 NTS neurons, which project to parvo-cellular PVH corticotrophin-releasing factor (CRF) neurons. CRF then causes the pituitary release of the adrenocorticotropic hormone to promote glucocorticoid production by the adrenal glands to suppress peripheral inflammation, i.e., the HPA axis.

In addition to this anti-inflammatory vagal afferent pathway, a second one, identified by the Tracey group in 2000, includes vagal afferents. This group demonstrated that stimulation of the distal end of the VN, i.e., vagal efferents, in rats prevented a septic LPS shock. VNS had an anti-TNFα effect as the necrosis factor-alpha (TNFα) in the liver, and blood tumor levels became dampened.These authors named this "Hat" mechanism assimilated to an "inflammatory reflex," i.e., a vago-vagal reflex where vagal afferents are activated by LPS-stimulated vagal efferents after central integration into the dorsal vagal complex. This group has also defined the macrophages involved in this effect as α7 nicotinic ACh receptors (α7nAChR). De Jonge et al. characterized the molecular function of this pathway involving α7 subunit- mediated Jak2-STAT3 macrophage activation, and Sun et al. showed that microRNA-124 is responsible for the CAP action by inhibiting the development of pro-inflammatory cytokines. The VN is not directly related to gut-resident macrophages but associates with enteric neurons expressing nNOS, VIP, and ChAT and situated next to these macrophages expressing the α7nAChR within the muscular.

Therefore, the VN has a dual anti-inflammatory function, both through its afferent and efferent fibers that stimulate the HPA axis and the CAP. The vagosplenic pathway is also an anti-inflammatory pathway.

7.3. The Vago-splenic pathway

Tracey's group has identified a vago-splenic pathway through the spleen, that is, a vago-sympathetic pathway. Classically the parasympathetic (i.e., in this case, the VN) and the sympathetic nervous systems have the opposite effect. Nevertheless, this result is synergistic in the vagosplenic system by a connection between the VN and the splenic nerve, a sympathetic nerve released by the celiac ganglion to activate the splenic nerve through the action of ACh on α7nAChR. The end result is to block the spleen production of TNFα. In comparison to the vagal neuronal cholinergic pathway, a non- neuronal cholinergic pathway is involved in this reaction. Yes, norepinephrine, activated by the splenic nerve, binds to spleen T-lymphocyte β2 receptors that release ACh that connects macrophage to α7nAChR to prevent the release of TNFα by these macrophages. These T-lymphocytes are located in the spleen's white pulp, particularly the central area receiving a dense noradrenergic innervation. There is an intermediate stage in contrast with the CAP, with a neuro-immune link affecting the splenic nerve and T- lymphocytes. The nature of this process is still contentious, however, as some scholars contend in favor of a system of direct compassion. By comparison, the Ghia group found that the CAP was triggered by intracerebroventricular injection of an M1 muscarinic ACh receptor agonist; vagotomy or splenic neurectomy reversed this effect. The same group found that the administration of galantamine, a key ACh-esterase receptor, activated the CAP and that vagotomy, splenic neurectomy, or splenectomy inhibited this effect. Nevertheless, Bellinger et al. documented a lack of evidence for cholinergic innervation of the rat spleen. Martelli et al. suggest that the CAP's efferent mediator is not the VN but the sympathetic nerve, that is to say, the splenic nerve. In addition, they found that vagotomy had little impact on the LPS-induced TNFα response when both splenic and splanchnic nerves were splanchnicectomy-activated and inhibited by LPS, raising the TNFα rates. They evoked an anti-inflammatory, splanchnic pathway. The mechanism used to activate the CAP and/or the splanchnic pathway was a septic shock caused by LPS in laboratory models of IBD and RA, which is rather distinct from other inflammatory situations in both works of the Tracey and Martelli group. However, there is no incompatibility between the function of a CAP and a splenic anti-inflammatory pathway when considering a vago-sympathetic pathway involving vagal afferents to the CAN and then descending pathways to stimulate sympathetic nerves.

The sympathetic spleen innervation modulates the lymphoid organ's cellular and humoral immune responses. In addition, the spleen-innervating noradrenergic fibers are in close contact with white pulp immune cells that express adrenergic receptors. The splenic preganglionic neurons in the thoracic and rostral lumbar spinal cord are regulated by a particular complex supra-spinal circuitry involved in controlling spleen neural-immune interactions. Upon central incorporation of its afferents in the CAN, the VN is able to modulate the sympathetic nervous system, which will then modulate the sympathetic nerves, such as the splenic nerve, by descending channels from the CAN, i.e., a vagosympathetic pathway.

7.4. The vago-sympathetic pathway

As mentioned above, vagal afferents end up in the NTS and activate the CAN from there, which in return is able to modulate the ANS by descending pathways that target the DMNV and the tractus intermediolateralis in the spinal cord at the origin of vagal and sympathetic afferents. Five CAN brain nuclei (i.e., PVH, noradrenergic group A5, caudal raphe area, rostral ventrolateral medulla, and ventromedial medulla) modulate sympathetic outflow through the innervation of intermediolateral cell column sympathetic neurons in the spinal cord. Thus, by increasing the sympathetic outflow, the VN may cause a ton-direct anti-inflammatory reflex. Among these brain structures,

Abe et al. has recently illuminated the function of the C1 adrenergic community and has demonstrated that these adrenergic neurons are involved in the stress-protective effect of renal ischemia-reperfusion injury by a sympathetic rather than a vagal pathway. Previously, this group had shown that activation of vagal afferents or efferents in mice 24 h before injury substantially decreased acute kidney inflammation and plasma levels of TNFα. Splenectomy suppressed this effect and mediated by α7nAChR- positive splenocytes. Only the PVH is able to modulate the ANS by its efferent projections to the DMNV and the sympathetic spinal preganglionic neurons. Stress through PVH CRF, for example, can inhibit DMNV, i.e., vagal afferents, and activate the sympathetic nervous system, i.e., sympathetic effect events. Recently, Deng et al. have demonstrated that chemical hypothalamus stimulation protects against colitis in rats via a central function of PVN, NTS, and VN. The ventrolateral pons ' noradrenergic nucleus A5 attacks the spinal intermediolateral column nearly entirely and is involved in controlling visceral sympathetic sound in rodents. A5 gets C1 Neuron inputs. The effect of a stimulus on sympathetic nerve function depends on the structure of the form of fibers. The relative value of each of these five regions may vary in regulating the sympathetic outflow. For eg, A5 > rostroventrolateral medulla > PVH, for the spleen. The A5 field is among the first regions to become contaminated after pseudorabies are inserted into the spleen. This area is therefore included in the reaction of all sympathetic-innervated organs. Multiple sympathetic targets must be linked to the A5 neurons. Specific areas may selectively inhibit sympathetic preganglionic neurons such as I the Barrington nucleus specifically involved in the regulation of parasympathetic outflow, (ii) the LC involved in stress and contributing to widespread sympathoadrenal activation in response to stressful stimuli, (iii) the periaqueductal white, lateral hypothalamus, A7 zone, NTS, Edinger-Westphal nucleon In the rostral ventrolateral medulla neurons increase their activation in combination with decreased sympathetic vasomotor reactions. Both of these findings show that sympathetic outflow is controlled differently by the supra-spinal regions, without a mechanism clearly defined. In fact, certain locations organize regional visceral reactions while making targeting individual circuits challenging.

7.5. How to target the Vagus nerve for anti-inflammatory properties?

The VN's anti-inflammatory properties may be targeted by pharmacology, enteral nutrition, VNS, supplementary medicines, or physical exercise.

Pharmacological Stimulation of the CAP

Pharmacological stimulation can be achieved either directly or peripherally by hitting the CAP.

Galantamine, a blocker of cholinesterase and a nicotinic receptor agonist, including α7nAChR, is capable of crossing the blood-brain barrier, activating the central cholinergic pathway and stimulating VN efferents. This medicine is used to treat Alzheimer's disease. Galantamine significantly inhibits the distribution of TNFα, whichIL-6, which increases survival in a model of murine endotoxemia. Consequently, galantamine may be used as an immune suppressant drug. Galantamine has, to our understanding, been used only in human inflammation but not in clinical studies. In the same way, CNI-1493 prevents the activation of the TNFα p38 MAPK pathway. Central injection of CNI-1493 significantly reduced serum TNFα levels during endotoxemia, and this effect is mediated by the VN (9). During a randomized trial, patients diagnosed with two doses of CNI-1493 for two weeks with Crohn's disease (CD) reported a randomized relapse and an endoscopic recovery of up to 45 percent of the patients involved (78).

Peripheral α7nAChR can be activated by agonists such as GTS-21, which was used in experimental human endotoxemia in a double-blind placebo control study. Good participants got a small dose of LPS after either the GTS-21 or placebo. The group treated with GTS-21 exhibited lower plasma levels of TNFα, IL-6, and IL-1ra compared to placebo (79). Pretreatment with GTS-21 greatly reduced the severity of pancreatitis (80) in mice after an experimental pancreatitis. Another α7nAChR agonist, AR-R17779, blocked a POI test for the mouse (81).

Nutritional CAP activation

In a hemorrhagic shock model, enteral feeding with a high-fat diet causes the release of cholecystokinin (CCK), which is known to stimulate vagal afferent CCK1 receptors and dampens the inflammatory response (TNFα, IL-6) via a vago-vagal anti-inflammatory reflex. In a study, CCK, vagotomy, and nicotinic receptor antagonists blocked high-fat enteral nutrition's beneficial effect on intestinal permeability. Mucosal mast cells are targets of the dietary anti-inflammatory vagal reflex, as lipid-rich enteral feeding has stopped the degranulation of the mucosal mast cells. A high-fat enteral diet may also be used in treating IBD, where TNFα and inflammation of the intestinal barrier are common. Enteral feeding, which is conventionally used in the treatment of an IBD outbreak, has proven its efficacy in causing clinical recovery in CD.

Complementary medications

Inflammatory bowel disorders are chronic crippling conditions that have an impact on the quality of life, and therapies are not necessarily successful and are not without side effects. Therefore, doctors use alternative drugs sometimes. Cramer et al. recently evaluated the effectiveness and health of yoga conducted at therapeutic withdrawal 90 min a week for 12 weeks to improve the quality of life of UC patients. The yoga group (n=39) had a slightly higher disease-specific quality of life at 12 and 24 weeks of follow- up, and disease incidence was lower at 24 weeks, relative to the published self-care treatment group (controls, n=38). Good-directed hypnotherapy in patients with IBS is well known to help. Keefer et al. performed seven gut- directed hypnosis sessions in 26 UC patients in clinical recovery and 29 patients with treatment control; the patients were followed up for one year. Patients in the hypnosis group continued in remission for longer than the control group at one year (68 vs. 40 percent). No important impact on other psychological factors (quality of life, attention to medicine, perceived stress) was found. The triggering of the CAP may be one pathway by which supplemental medicines will strengthen IBD. Both acupuncture and yoga decrease heart rate and the production of inflammatory cytokines. The increase in vagal tone mediates the influence. Upon administration of LPS in mice, acupuncture will decrease TNFα release. Acupuncture is associated with spleen-related down-regulation of TNFα synthesis, which was reversed by splenic neurectomy and vagotomy. Hypnosis modifies the amplitude in heart rhythm (HRV) by increasing parasympathetic movement and lowering the sympathetic tone. Yoga and meditation on mindfulness improve movement in the vagus. Thus, these alternative drugs may be of use in the care of patients with IBD via the Lock.

Vagus Nerve Stimulation

The Corning JL was the first to use VNS for epilepsy control in the 1880s. The method was then forgotten but was reintroduced by Bailey and Bremer in 1938. In 1990, the very first VNS for the treatment of pharmacoresistant epilepsy was presented in humans, and VNS was approved for this purpose by the US Food and Drug Administration (FDA) in 1994 and for Europe in 1997. The FDA approved VNS in 2005 for treating pharmacoresistant disorder. VNS has currently diagnosed ~100,000 patients with autism, and ~5,000 patients with depression (Livanova, Houston, TX, USA).

The antiepileptic and therapeutic effects of VNS can be readily explained from the first relay in the NTS by the extensive predictions of the VN in the head. VNS's mode of action is not yet fully known, but evidence advocates for LC, thalamus, hippocampus, periaqueductal white and neocortex (98) functions. If in the antiepileptic action of VNS, the role of vagal afferent C- fibers was evoked, their modification by capsaicin did not counteract the action, arguing for a function of vagal A-and B-fibers. Classically, five VNS parameters are used: amplitude (0.5–3.5 mA), frequency (20–30 Hz), pulse duration (250–500 µs), and service period 30 s ON and 5 min OFF. Frequencies of 2–300 Hz caused electroencephalographic desynchronization of the "encéphale isolé" cat, which was dampened by a cervical end ligature of the VN while favoring the position of vagal afferent fibers. The effectiveness of VNS is frequency-dependent to a maximum level of 50 Hz above which a VN harm is caused. In rodents, the VNS (parameters of stimulus used for epilepsy) causes neuronal activity in the brain region implicated in inducing seizures. In human studies of brain imaging, improvements were identified in regions receiving supra-medullar projections afferent to VN. VNS is a slow-acting treatment because, after two years, a drop in epilepsy occurs in 50 percent of patients. Elliott et al. demonstrated a time-dependent decrease in epilepsy in 65 epileptic patients with a 10-year median duration of the VNS. In fact, the positive impact of VNS at six months and 1, 2, 4, 6, 8, and 10 years was respectively 35.7, 52.1, 58.3, 60.4, 65.7, 75.5, and 75.5 percent.

Stimulation of the nerve vagus can be performed via the skin invasively or non-invasively. Invasive VNS is usually conducted by a neurosurgeon under general anesthesia, and an electrode is wound around the left cervical VN in the neck subcutaneously attached by a cord to a pulse generator situated in the left thoracic wall. Implant lasts roughly one h. VNS is classically conducted on the left VN, which innervates the heart's atrioventricular node while the right VN innervates the sinoatrial node, therefore providing a lower heart rate effect (108). The VNS is made by Livanova, a combination of Cyberonics and Sorin (Houston, Tex, USA), and consisting of a pair of helical electrodes (2 or 3 mm in diameter), a battery-powered generator, a tunneling tool, software and programming resources (www.livanova.com/). The price of the pulse generator (model 102) plus the electrode (model 302) is~9,300 euros. Security and tolerability of implantable VNS are demonstrated. The mild adverse effects recorded by the patients include: speech change, cough, dyspnea, paresthesia, diarrhea, headache, and pain; these adverse events worsen over time and are easily managed by decreasing pressure severity. The battery life relies on the level of stimuli used and is higher than the high frequency (20–30 Hz) for low frequency (5–10 Hz), e.g.,~5–10 years.

Based on the idea that the CAP includes the vagal nerve's parasympathetic outflow, VNS is conducted at the lowest frequencies (1–5–10 Hz) to achieve the anti-inflammatory effect. In rats with cervical vagotomy, Borovikova et al. conducted low frequency (1 Hz) VNS and induced distal end cutting off the VN while inducing vagal afferents. Bernik et al., who conducted VNS of the left or right VN in anesthetized rats, showed that endotoxin-induced hypotension was avoided by a 20 min stimulation.

Non-invasive VNS (n-VNS) involves no surgical implantation and improves VNS protection and tolerability. Another such strategy is the transcutaneous auricular VNS (ta-VNS). Nonetheless, the VN contains a tactile "auricular" component, of which the cymbal concha of the external ear and the NTS ventures of cats and humans are inherited. Ta-VNS shows the same perceptual and behavior results as VNS. This affects the vagal core projections as done at 25 Hz in healthy people, as opposed to an earlobe control stimulation. And the auricular-vagal reflex can be clarified by the close anatomical relation between auricular concha, VN, NTS, and DMNV. The anti-inflammatory pathway may also be activated by ta-VNS. In keeping with this neuroanatomic principle, ta-VNS suppresses LPS-induced inflammatory responses in rats through α7nAChR, and this effect was suppressed after vagotomy or with antagonist α7nAChR injection.

There are actually two n-VNS machines that are used for anxiety, insomnia, and headache, but they may also be used in GI tract inflammatory conditions such as IBD, IBS, and POI and others. The Cerbomed system called NEMOS (Erlangen, Germany) uses an intra-auricular electrode (like an earpiece) to activate the vagal auricular division, and in 2011, it obtained European approval for the indication of Epilepsia. This system is available in Germany, Austria, Italy, Switzerland, and the UK. The ideal stimulus is selected by the patients based on the severity to experience a non-painful stinging with a prescribed stimulus period of 4 h a day, following nine months of ta-VNS, a 70 percent decrease in seizure incidence was reported, and a 43 percent decrease was reported in another test following eight weeks. It has been shown that ta-VNS improves HRV and decreases sympathetic outflow in devices. The second system is referred to as GammaCore (electroCore LLC, Basking Ridge, NJ, USA) and consists of a compact stimulator and two circular stainless steel disks that serve as skin touch surfaces to provide the cervical vagal nerve with a locked, low-voltage electrical signal; In another study, mean pain scores in patients with chronic migraine were decreased significantly at two h from baseline. GammaCore is currently being tested in randomized trials in patients with primary headache conditions in North America and EU countries. N-VNS with a Gammacore system reduces cytokines and chemokines produced from whole blood culture in healthy volunteers. No major adverse effects related to the system with NEMOS and Gammacore have been recorded. Compared to invasive VNS, n-VNS has its conformity drawback and is a significant issue in the management of chronic inflammatory diseases.

Physical exercise An ANS disorder, with weak vagal function and high emotion, coincides with various medical disorders such as arrhythmia, heart disease, and hypertension, and damage. High rates of cardiorespiratory preparation also reduce cardiovascular morbidity and mortality and inflammation. There is a negative association between cardiorespiratory activity and cardiovascular injuries, which is mediated in part by inflammatory factors. The Ants in middle-aged people is known to affect the relationship between cardiorespiratory health and inflammation. Physical activity and fitness preparation will also have a calming impact on the CAP, as RR variation is inversely related to inflammatory markers. Daily physical activity causes a rise in vagal resting sound, which decreases central 5-HT production, in which central 5-HT improves vagal regulation in aware rats.

7.8. Vagus Nerve in the modulation of inflammatory disorder conditions

The VN has the potential to modulate inflammatory factors, depending on its activation of the HPA axis and the CAP. Experimental and more recent clinical results, including pilot trials in the IBD, RA, and POI realms, are available for this effect. We'll focus on inflammatory GI diseases such as IBD, IBS, and POI in the next lineup.

Chronic inflammatory bowel conditions CD and ulcerative colitis (UC) classically reflect inflammatory bowel diseases. CD includes both of the digestive tract and ano-perineal region, while recto-colon is included in UC. IBD begins from 15 to 30 years and is marked by periodic flares and remissions. During outbreaks, patients undergo many intestinal and extra- intestinal symptoms such as stomach discomfort, vomiting, face, hair, or swelling of the joints, thereby illustrating their major effect on IBD patients ' quality of life. Both the CD and UC have a heterogeneous nature history. Around 1.5 million Americans and 2.2 million Europeans are affected by IBD, and due to the "Westernization" of our culture, the frequency and prevalence of IBD is growing. Pathophysiology of IBD includes immunological, genetic, and environmental causes. Experimental and clinical evidence tends to manifest the role of stress in IBD pathophysiology. Classically, stress improves bowel permeability, modifies intestinal microbiota, and immunity, which are factors implicated in IBD's pathophysiology. The VN is interested in the impacts of pressures on the digestive tract. Pain reduces the VN classically and activates the sympathetic nervous system (66). Chronic stress is more involved in the pathophysiology of IBD as well as other GI conditions such as IBS, rather than acute stress (132). Stress causes an imbalanced ANS with a blunted sympathetic operation in CD (133) and a vagal dysfunction in UC (134) as recorded in IBD. Earlier, we reported a relationship between an imbalanced ANS, psychological change (3), and pro-inflammatory profiles (135) in IBD patients. Currently, hormones, immunosuppressants (thiopurines, methotrexate), biologics (anti-TNFα, anti-adhesion molecule, anti-IL12/23) constitute standard treatment of IBD patients. The therapeutic aim is not only to relieve IBD-related symptoms but also to encourage mucosal healing as it has been implicated in a superior long-term prognosis including lower surgical risk, hospitalizations, and systemic steroid requirements (136). Anti- TNFα therapies have improved the IBD prognosis, but 10 percent -40 percent of patients lose reaction within 12 months (137) and another 10–20 percent annually afterward (138). Additionally, these therapies are not free of side effects (139), so drug adherence is a problem in patients with IBD (140). Seventy percent of CD patients and 35 percent of UC patients (141) undergo IBD surgery. The surgical procedure is done in the case of medical care loss or complications, and patients are re-operated as surgery is not curative but only suspensive, but even medical treatment is. IBD is often detected late at a time when lesions such as stenosis, fistula, CD abscesses, and more refractory to medical diagnosis, are emerging. Consequently, it is of concern to treat IBD early when the disease is solely inflammatory. These patients also have the risk of recto-colonic cancer due to chronic inflammation, and actually, mucosal healing is a gold standard in IBD care.

Experimental CAP-potentiating VN anti-inflammatory activity was documented in experimental colitis (142, 143), vagotomy (142), VNS (144, 145), and peripheral or main AChesterase inhibitors (146). Its anti- inflammatory function goes through a pathway involving nicotinic receptors that is dependent on the macrophage. Many counter-inflammatory pathways do play a part, however, when vagal integrity is impaired, and its defensive function does not play.

Classically, low frequency (5–10 Hz) VNS activates vagal afferents, that is, CAP. Nevertheless, we have shown in laboratory conditions that vagal afferents are often triggered in anesthetized rats under VNS in an fMRI test using complex causal modeling to approximate neuronal integration, also at low-frequency stimulation. We have stated that, in a CD patient under VNS, long-term low frequency (10 Hz) VNS was able to cause changes in the electroencephalogram. In addition, both stimulation of vagal afferent and efferent fibers is of importance in the neuroanatomic sense of the pathways that are involved in the VN's anti-inflammatory role.

By Using VNS in a rat model of TNBS colitis classically used for CD, It is shown for five consecutive days, low frequency (5 Hz) chronic VNS performed with parameters classically used for epilepsy enhanced colitis. Indeed, a multiparametric index of colitis has been improved in rats under VNS, taking into account clinical, biological, macroscopic, and histological damage, as well as pro-inflammatory cytokines. We observed that VNS was more effective with less inflammation located directly above the main inflammatory lesion on the lesion region. Sun et al. have tested the chronic VNS effect in the same experimental colitis model by using physiological, histological, and biochemical parameters with a higher frequency stimulus (20 Hz) on colonic inflammation. They also reported HRV under VNS in rats suffering from colitis. They reported a substantial decline in colitis under the cytokines VNS andIL-6 and TNF-α and saw an increase in the sympathovagal balance. More recently, in a related strategy, Jin et al., using the same TNBS colitis model, found that chronic VNS enhanced colonic inflammation by inhibiting pro-inflammatory cytokines via the autonomic mechanism; applying non-invasive electroacupuncture to VNS increased the anti-inflammatory effect of VNS.

Clinical

Until recently, there were a few evidence available on the VN's anti- inflammatory function in IBD. However, vagal tone monitoring and sympathovagal equilibrium using HRV, a robust non-invasive method that quantifies sympathetic and parasympathetic behaviors, enables such an approach. The risk of contracting a chronic disease is linked with a dysregulated ANS with a decreased vagal tone. HRV testing is an important method in the sense of brain-visceral activity that allows for the sensing of vagal tone and its weakness, and hence the CAP deficit. HRV screening is a biomarker that measures several chronic inflammatory disease prognoses. As we know, a reduction in vagal tone causes a decline in HRV. In IBD patients, we have shown a link between vagal tone and emotional change (low negative emotions vs. high negative emotions) and how patients coped with their disease. A good coping profile was correlated with low CD vagal tone and high UC vagal tone. Accordingly, distinguishing IBD patients by disease (CD vs. UC) as well as the influence of psychological influences on vagal tone is significant. Furthermore, recent studies have indicated an autonomic malfunction underlying RA production. We also recorded that CD patients with low vagal resting tone had higher levels of TNFα in the blood and salivary cortisol than patients with high vagal tone. Therefore a weak vagal tone is linked to a pro-inflammatory condition. Therefore, given that stress reduces the VN and therefore prefers a pro-inflammatory condition, this may justify, at least in part, the stress in patients with IBD can support a relapse. In this sense, monitoring of resting vagal tone over time can be useful (a) to assess the fragile state, (b) to recommend appropriate behavioral treatment such as holistic medication, proven to promote VN, CAP pharmacological intervention, or VNS to restore natural vagal tone, and (c) to monitor the treatment efficacy of the parasympathetic mechanism.

We conducted a pilot VNS analysis in a translational approach in patients with CD, where seven patients with active ileocolonic CD were implanted with a VNS system. Just two out of seven patients were on inclusion for diagnosis (Azathioprine). Clinical (Crohn's disease activity index, CDAI), biological (CRP, fecal calprotectin), endoscopic (Crohn's disease endoscopic intensity index, CDEIS) activity markers were identified during a follow-up span of 6 months. The first patient inserted was April 2012, and November 2014 was the 7th patient. In a follow-up analysis, all the patients joined. In five of the seven cases, VNS caused intense remission. Following a 3-month VNS, two patients were taken off the study and transferred to infliximab and azathioprine, one (Ileo-cecal resection) was surgeries. These two patients have the highest CDAI, CRP, and CDEIS on inclusion, which indicates that VNS is more suggested in mild CD as a slow-acting treatment. Both patients kept the unit in place with the task cycle still operating, except for one of the two patients with low stimulation amplitude (0.5 mA) excluded from the sample. VNS has been well accepted with the classic minor side effect, basically described by heaviness. We have had no local or systemic infection problem, and no VNS unit has been removed. Recently, the results on the first seven patients were recorded for the first time after a6-month follow-up (152). Also, VNS may be used to sustain drug-induced remission. Surgery is used to treat CD lesions, and VNS as a slow-acting treatment can be an important method to reduce postoperative CD recurrence.

Irritable bowel syndrome

The major symptoms of IBS include irritable bowel syndrome, Stomach pain, bloating, and changed bowel behavior without any endogenous origin with a greater incidence in women. In industrialized countries, the prevalence of IBS ranges from 10 to 15 percent and represents up to 12 percent of primary care doctors and 28 percent of gastroenterologist medical visits. The key effects of IBS are major loss in quality of life, days off work, and a substantial increase in healthcare costs. Patients classically experience extra-intestinal signs such as vomiting, arthralgia, gastrointestinal disorders, anxiety, and fatigue in conjunction with digestive symptoms. Fibromyalgia, also related to IBS, aggravates digestive symptoms. Psychological factors, such as anxiety or major depression, are often found in patients with IBS (up to 50 percent). Pain has an important part to play in IBS pathophysiology. In particular, in 30–50 percent of patients, early life trauma such as a history of emotional, sexual, or physical abuse is reported, and symptoms are often triggered by stress. Of IBS patients are frequently diagnosed with intestinal distension- induced gastrointestinal hypersensitivity and distinguished by lower pain levels which are a typical predictor of the condition. Mechanisms of this visceral hypersensitivity tend to be explained by low-grade inflammation in the GI tract (which may support neuronal plasticity modifications) and mast cell sensitization at intestinal afferent endpoints. 4–30 percent of post-infectious IBS is associated with bacterial gastroenteritis. Nevertheless, at the time of diagnosis, anxiety, high levels of interpersonal stress, somatization, and pessimistic attitudes about disease were also predictors of post-infectious IBS, calling for an IBS cognitive-behavioral model. IBS has been contrasted with an IBD "minima" because of increased numbers of gut mucosal T-lymphocytes and mast cells, as well as increased levels of blood pro- inflammatory cytokines(IL-10andIL-12, indicating Th1 polarization), were identified. Overall, IBS is characterized as a biopsychosocial paradigm due to a blunted brain–a good axis associated with an up-regulation between the gut and the brain in neural processing. Patients are hypervigilant about their signs that describe the hypersensitivity of visceral. Among IBS cases, central sensory systems are affected, and this is assimilated into a condition of extreme sensitization. Dysautonomia, a brain-gut dysfunction marker, has been identified as having a high sympathetic and low parasympathetic sound, independent of positive or negative affective change. Because of IBS ' multifactorial pathophysiology, its therapeutic diagnosis is ineffective and based primarily on pain relief. Psychotherapy, such as cognitive-behavioral therapy and alternative treatment such as hypnosis, is known to boost vagal tone, which may be of use in treating symptoms of IBS.

From a pathophysiological viewpoint, IBS is of interest to attack both the GI tract and the central nervous system through the VN. VNS will be of great importance in IBS therapy based on its peripheral anti-inflammatory activity through the CAP and its main role as an antidepressant. Furthermore, the VN is involved in pain control, and it has been shown that VNS modifies core pain perception. Indeed, VNS has been shown to raise the pain threshold in rat visceral pain models and to modulate affective memory related to visceral pain. Changes in VNS pain have also been documented in epileptic patients, probably by regulation of peripheral nociceptor activity. Deep breathing improves the cardiac vagal sound and inhibits the production in healthy volunteers of acid-induced oesophageal hypersensitivity; this effect was eliminated by atropine. For stable volunteers with ta-VNS, the somatic pain levels are raised. VNS stimulates vagal afferents involved in the reducing inhibitory regulation of pain extending to brain nuclei.

There are currently no published reports on VNS management of IBS, but two trials that use n-VNS are listed in ClinicalTrial.gov. ElectroCore LLC has set up the first test, with a new n-device called GammaCore. A randomized, single-center, double-blind, concurrent, sham-controlled pilot trial applies to the diagnosis of clinical dyspepsia or IBS symptoms. No reports have yet been released, even though completed. The second report, also recruiting, examines the impact of a 6-month transcutaneous VNS on intestinal and systemic inflammation, mucosal permeability of the intestinal transit period, and quality of life in patients with IBS. It will have ten IBS women aged between 18 and 60.

Postoperative ileus

Abdominal surgery causes POI anywhere the surgical site is located. A delayed gastric emptying and prolonged intestinal transit are known as POI. Stomach and small intestine functions return to normal within 24–48 hours while the colon usually takes longer (up to 72 hours). GI motility recovery will take longer hospitalization times and, thus, higher healthcare costs. In the US, the cost of this postoperative complication was calculated at US$ 1 billion / year. Sympathy-adrenergic and nonadrenergic vagal noncholinergic efferent pathways play a part in the POI processes, while capsaicin-sensitive neurons are active in the afferent reflex pathway. Supra-spinal brain nuclei, in particular common hypothalamic and pontine-medullary neurons implicated in the autonomic modulation of GI activity, have also been implicated in POI. A function for CRF is evoked in the PVH since CRF is a key mediator in the GI tract stress response. In addition, stress is well known to impede gastric emptying, as demonstrated by intracerebroventricular injection of a-helical CRF-, a CRF antagonist, which decreases the delay in gastric emptying under stress conditions. The effect is dependent on the receptor for CRF1. More recently, a peripheral pathway was identified, involving the CAP in the POI process. Yes, abdominal surgery causes muscular propria inflammation and activation of resident macrophages that produce TNFα. Depletion and inactivation of the macrophage muscular network avoids POI. Systemic administration of both active nACh agonists and VNS decreases inflammatory response to bowel interference during surgery. The CAP induces this anti-inflammatory reaction, which is mediated by a reduction in macrophage activation and cytokine production. Gum chewing decreases POI by promoting activity in the vagus. Thus targeting the CAP could improve POI by its anti-inflammatory action, and therefore VNS could be a potential treatment for preventing POI.

De Jonge et al. demonstrated in a mouse model of intestinal manipulation that 5 min of cervical VNS before abdominal surgery increased GI transit by alpha7 subunit-mediated Jak2-STAT3 activation in intestinal macrophages, suggesting that VNS that represent a new therapeutic approach to shortening POI. Stenberg et al. recently explored the therapeutic efficacy of VNS in patients undergoing abdominal colorectal cancer treatment, randomized to group placebo stimulation (n= 5), 5 Hz stimulation (n= 6), or 20 Hz stimulation (n= 7). At the beginning and at the end of the procedure, they conducted 1 ms and 2.5 mA during 2 min of VNS. They found that, in patients, abdominal VNS greatly decreased the production of LPS-induced IL8 and IL6 by whole blood. In the same analysis, they found that in a murine model of POI, abdominal VNS was as effective as cervical VNS.

Conclusion

The VN exerts an anti-inflammatory effect through the HPA axis and the CAP. There is also a vagosympathetic anti-inflammatory pathway where the VN and the sympathetic system (i.e., the splenic nerve) function synergistically. This anti-inflammatory effect involves both afferent vagal and efferent fibers. VN therapy provides new clinical pathways for inflammatory GI disorders such as IBD, POI, IBS, and other TNFα-mediated illnesses such as RA or psoriasis. Among other therapeutic methods, VNS, either invasive or non-invasive, emerges in the Bioelectronic Medicine age

(184) as an important method with no significant side effects. Continued condition patients are open to this non-drug treatment because they are generally resistant to traditional treatments, in particular, due to their side effects and the need for continued use of such treatments.

Chapter 8: Vagus Nerve as Modulator of brain - psychiatric disorders (Depression, Anxiety, Trauma and PTSD) and intestinal disorders

The vagus nerve is the main part of the parasympathetic nervous system that controls a wide variety of vital body functions, including mood control, immune response, metabolism, and heart rate. It establishes one of the linkages between the brain and the gastrointestinal tract and sends information to the brain about the condition of the internal organs via afferent fibers. In this review article, we discuss various vagus nerve roles that make it an attractive target in the treatment of psychological and gastrointestinal disorders. Preliminary evidence is that activation of the vagus nerve is a promising potential therapy for medication-refractory depression, posttraumatic stress disorder, and inflammatory bowel disease. Treatments that target the vagus nerve increases the vagal tone and inhibit the development of cytokines. Both are important resistance tool. It is stimulating vagal afferent fibers in the gut influences monoaminergic brain systems in the brain stem, which play key roles in major psychiatric conditions, such as mood and anxiety disorders. Inline, there is tentative evidence that gut bacteria have beneficial effects on depression and anxiety, inter alia by affecting the vagus nerve function. Since the vagal tone is associated with the capacity to control stress responses and can be affected through breathing, its improvement by meditation and yoga is likely to lead to tolerance and reduction of symptoms of depression and anxiety.

8.1. Vagus Nerve and self-help exercises for anxiety depression, trauma and PTSD

Vagus nerve self-help exercise help in following ways:

- Turn on neurogenesis, which allows our brains to sprout new cells.
- Quickly shut off pain, hyper-arousal and fight / flight with a calming response.
- Memories sharpen.\Fight infectious diseases.
- Enable it to tolerate high blood pressure.
- Block hormone cortisol and other oxidizing agents which age and deteriorate the brain and body
- Block systemic (body-wide) inflammation-a major factor behind aging and poor health.
- Help us conquer the fear and depression.
- Help us to sleep well.
- Heighten the human growth hormone levels.
- Help us to improve insulin resistance and suppressing allergic reactions.
- Lower risk of developing headaches from fatigue and anxiety. Help save and expand our mitochondria-this is a secret to keeping our energy levels optimum and not damaging our DNA and RNA.
- Influences our general desire to lead fuller, happier and more active lives.

Stimulation of the vagus nerve can be quickly activated by a variety of relaxing and calming techniques:

- Deep / slow relaxing in the abdomen.
- 'OM' Chanting
- Cold water face immersion during exercise
- Fill the mouth with saliva and submerge the tongue to induce a vagal hyper-relaxation reflex.
- Loud gargling of saliva
- Loud humming
- Inhale through your nose and exhale from your mouth to practice deep breathing.
- Slowly breathe.
- Breathe harder

Breathing exercises

You will learn how to use relaxation techniques to move the mind away from discomfort. One thing the human mind explores at a time. When you concentrate on the rhythm of your breathing, the pain is not your concern. Many of us appear to stop breathing the moment we fear discomfort and hold our breath. Breath keeping stimulates the reaction to fight / flight / freeze, which helps to increase the sensation of discomfort, weakness, anxiety or terror. You may continue as follows: take a deep inhalation (i.e. extending your diaphragm) through your abdomen to the count of five, pause, and then gradually exhale through a small opening in your chest. While most people take about 10 to 14 breaths per minute at rest. To enter parasympathetic / relaxation / healing mode, lowering the pulse to 5-7 periods a minute is best. Exhaling from your mouth rather than nose makes your breathing more like a deliberate operation which lets you to readily track your body.

When you lower your breaths every minute and get into parasympathetic mode, your muscles will relax, lowering your anxieties and worries. The delivery of oxygen to the cells of the body is increasing and this helps to generate endorphins, the feel-good hormones of the body. For decades, Tibetan monks have been doing' conscious breathing' so nothing is unique about it. Through pretending you inhale IN passion, you will deepen the feeling, and exhale OUT appreciation. Such ancient methods will also enhance memory, fight fatigue, reduce blood pressure or heart rate and strengthen the immune systems — and it's safe!

'OM' Chanting

The International Journal of Yoga conducted a fascinating review in 2011, where' OM' chanting was contrasted with the pronunciation of' SSS' as well as a rest state to decide if chanting is more relaxing to the vagus nerve. The study showed the chanting was significantly more effective than either the pronunciation of the' sss' or the state of rest.

Active' OM' chanting is associated with the experience of a sense of stimulation in the ears and all over the body. Such a feeling is also supposed to be conveyed via the vagus nerve's auricular branch, which to cause limbic (HPA axis) deactivation. How to chant? Keep the' OM' part of the vowel (o) for 5 seconds then proceed for the next 10 seconds through the consonant (m) part. Holding chanting for ten minutes. Complete with a deep sigh, and finish with appreciation.

Cool Water Physical exercise

This induces a rise in sympathetic activation (HPA axis-fight / flight, stress response), coupled with parasympathetic withdrawal (rest, digestion, regeneration, immune system), resulting in higher heart rate (HR). Research have shown that cold water face immersion tends to be an easy and successful way of promoting parasympathetic reactivation through the vagus nerve directly after exercise, enhancing heart rate reduction, intestinal motility, and turning the immune system on. The activation of the vagus nerve is also successful in a non-exercise environment. Subjects stayed seated in ice-water face immersion and bent their head slightly into a bath of cool water. The skin is covered in such a way that the nose, eyebrows and at least two-thirds of both cheeks are inundated. Water temperatures were set at 10- 12 °C.

Increases salivation

The calmer the mind and the stronger the stimulation, the quicker the salivation becomes to induce. You know that the vagus nerve has been activated and the body is in parasympathetic mode because the mouth can emit copious quantities of saliva.

Start relaxing and reclining in a chair to induce salivation, and picture a juicy lemon. Just rest your tongue in this bath while your mouth fills with saliva (if that doesn't happen, just fill your mouth with a tiny amount of warm water and rest your tongue in this bath. Just relaxing will induce saliva secretion). Relax more now, and feel both the legs, feet, knees, neck back and head relaxed. Breathe this feeling profoundly, and live here for as long as you can.

8.2. Vagus related treatment of Depression and Anxiety

Basic Depression Pathophysiology

Major depressive disorder ranks among the leading contributors to global disease risk on mental health (104). With a median frequency of 1.0% (Czech Republic) to 16.9% (US) (105), the cost of depression poses a significant economic burden on our society (106). Depression pathophysiology is diverse and involves social, environmental stress factors, genetic and biological pathways, such as the HPA axis overdrive, inflammation (31), and monoamine neurotransmission disruptions, as mentioned above (91). For instance, a lack of tryptophan amino acid, which is a precursor to serotonin, may cause depressive symptoms such as depressed mood, depression, and hopelessness.

The overdrive of the HPA axis is observed more often in individuals with more extreme (i.e., melancholic or psychotic) disorder, where the inhibitory functions of cortisol input become disrupted, leading to cytokine oversecretion (107). Chronic sensitivity to elevated inflammatory cytokines has been shown to induce depression (108). It may be clarified by the fact that cytokine overexpression results in a drop in serotonin levels (109). In line with this, anti-inflammatory drug therapy has the ability to decrease depressive symptoms (110). In particular, IBD is an important risk factor for disturbances of mood and anxiety (111), and these medical symptoms raise the risk of IBD exacerbation (112).

VNS in depression

In people with treatment-resistant disorder, a European multicenter study found a significant effect of VNS on depressive symptoms. The 3-month implementation of VNS resulted in a response rate of 37% and a remission rate of 17%. The response rate reached 53 percent after one year of therapy, and the relapse rate reached 33 percent. A meta-analysis comparing VNS procedure to the normal care in suicidal patients found a response rate of about 50 percent in the acute phase of the disorder and a 20 percent long-term remission rate after two years of therapy. Indeed, several other studies have demonstrated the long-term effect of VNS in chronic treatment-resistant depression. In fact, a5-year retrospective observational analysis evaluating drug outcomes as normal and VNS as adjunctive therapy only in medication- resistant depression as normal reported a greater health outcome and a higher risk of recovery in the VNS community. That was also the case with comorbid depression and anxiety patients who are chronic non-responders with antidepressant drug trials. It is important to remember that both of these experiments were open-label and did not use a randomized sample design controlled by placebo.

Patients of depression showed increased concentrations of proinflammatory cytokines in blood and cerebrospinal fluid. The benefit of VNS in depression may be due to inhibitory activity on proinflammatory cytokine production and marked peripheral rises in anti-inflammatory circulating cytokines. Additionally, improvement after VNS was consistent with altered CRH secretion, thereby stopping the HPA axis from overdrive. Changed development and secretion of CRH may result from a direct stimulatory effect, transmitted from the vagus nerve via the NTS to the hypothalamus paraventricular nucleus. Finally, peripheral blood production of TNF-α has been shown to inhibit VNS, which is increased in psychiatric depression.

Nutritional effect Anxiety symptoms

The gut microbiota is the possible primary modulator of the immune system and the nervous system. Targeting it may lead to greater change in the mental symptoms of stressed or nervous patients. There is growing evidence that dietary components such as probiotics, gluten, as well as medications such as anti-oxidant agents and antibiotics, by interfering with the gut microbiota, have a strong influence on vagus nerve function and that this effect differs significantly amongst individuals. In addition, animal experiments have shown that microbiota contact with the brain includes the vagus nerve, and this interaction can lead to mediating effects on the brain and, consequently, actions. Lactobacillus-species, for example, has gained considerable attention because of their use as probiotics and health-promoting properties. Bravo et al. showed that repeated treatment of mice with Lactobacillus rhamnosus (strain B-1) resulted in decreased rates of stress-induced corticosterone and actions comparable to anxiety and depression. The recurrent diagnosis of L has been proven to be. Rhamnosus (JB-1) mediated region-dependent shifts in GABA(B1b) mRNA in the brain with rises in cortical (cellular and prelimbic) regions and concomitant declines in expression in hippocampus, amygdala and LC zones. Alternatively, L. Rhamnosus (JB-1) decreased GABA(Aα2) mRNA production in the prefrontal cortex and amygdala but enhanced GABA(Aα2) in the hippocampus, counteracting the traditional pathogenesis of depressive symptoms: loss of pre-frontal regulation and overactivity in subcortical, anxiogenic brain regions. Notable, L. Rhamnosus (JB-1) decreased corticosterone stress-induced, and activity linked to anxiety and depression. It is not unexpected because the pathogenesis of anxiety and depression includes changes in central GABA receptor expression. The effects of L on an antidepressant and anxiolytic In vasectomized mice, rhamnosus was not detected, defining the vagus as a significant modulatory, constitutive signaling channel between the bacteria exposed to the gut and the brain. In line with this, the anxiolytic effect obtained with Bifidobacterium longum therapy in a model of chronic colitis associated with anxiety-like activity was absent in mice that were vasectomized before colitis induction.

In humans, psychobiotics, due to their antidepressant and anxiolytic activity, a genus of probiotics with anti-inflammatory properties may be effective for treating patients with psychiatric disorders. Differences in gut microbiota composition have been shown in people with depression as opposed to healthy individuals. Importantly, the fecal samples collected into germ-free mice from five patients with depression culminated in suicidal behavior.

Influence of calming strategies on depressive symptoms

It has been found that self-generated positive emotions by loving-kindness therapy contribute to an increase in positive emotions compared to the control group, an effect moderated by baseline vagal tone. In effect, increased positive emotions created vagal tone changes that are possibly influenced by enhanced expectations of social relations. Individuals of depression, anxiety, and chronic pain have benefited from daily meditation carefulness preparation, showing a dramatic increase in the severity of the symptoms.

Controlled trials have found successful yoga-based approaches in the management of depression from minor depressive symptoms to major depressive disorder (MDD). Many yoga activities will specifically activate the vagus nerve by improving the vagal tone resulting in enhanced autonomic control, executive functions, and mood and stress management. The suggested neurophysiological pathways for efficacy in alleviating depressive symptoms by yoga-based treatments suggest that yoga breathing causes increased vagal tone. A lot of studies demonstrate the effects of yogic

meditation on brain activity and physiological parameters. Therefore, a breathing-based meditative procedure, Sudarshan Kriya Yoga (SKY) activates the vagus nerve and exerts various autonomic effects, including improvements in heart rate, increased memory, and improved bowel function. During SKY, a series of breathing techniques with various frequencies, intensities, distances, and with end-inspiratory and end-expiratory grips produces diverse sensations from different visceral afferents, sensory receptors, and baroreceptors. They potentially affect various vagal fibers, which, in effect, cause physiological changes in muscles, and affect the limbic system. New research found that even patients who did not respond to antidepressants reported a substantial decrease in symptoms of depression and anxiety relative to the control group after eight weeks of having an adjunctive therapy with SKY.

Yoga in people with depression has been shown to decrease depressive symptoms. Increased HRV is consistent with Iyengar yoga, which confirms the theory that yoga breathing and postures function in part by that parasympathetic speech.

8.3. Vagus nerve-related treatment of PTSD

VNS in PTSD

Nervous stimulation has shown potential in treatment-resistant anxiety conditions, including PTSD (8), as a therapeutic alternative. Chronic VNS has been shown to minimize rat anxiety (96) and increase scores in patients with treatment-resistant depression on the Hamilton Anxiety Scale (8). The vagus nerve sends impulses to the NTS when activated (162), and the NTS carries out direct representations to the amygdala and the hypothalamus. Additionally, VNS enhances the production of NE in the basolateral amygdala (163) and hippocampus and cortex (93). NE injection into the amygdala contributes to improved information about extinction (164). Thus, VNS may be a good method for growing the preservation of extinction. In rats, for example, extinction combined with VNS therapy will lead to remission of fear and changes in symptoms comparable to PTSD (151). In addition, VNS paired with extinction learning promotes plasticity between the prefrontal infralimbic medial cortex and the amygdala basolateral complex to promote the deletion of programmed fear responses (165). In fact, by inhibiting the sympathetic nervous system function (119), VNS can also promote extinction. An immediate reduction in anxiety caused by VNS may lead to VNS-driven extinction by interfering with the sympathetic response to the CS, breaking the CS connection with fear. However, the validity of these results includes randomized controlled trials. One of VNS's most consistent neurophysiological effects is to decrease hippocampal activity, possibly by improving GABAergic signaling (166). As mentioned above, the hippocampus is a vital component of the fear system, since it is a central organ in the encoding of episodic memory and space background. A number of other studies have reported reduced hippocampal activity after VNS in other disorders such as depression or schizophrenia.

Positive Effect of Nutrient Components on PTSD

Recent evidence shows that probiotics could have the ability to decrease inflammatory reactions and related effects triggered by stress. Exploratory research analyzing the microbiota of PTSD patients and controls subject to trauma showed a reduced presence of three strains of bacteria in PTSD patients: Actinobacteria, Lentisphaerae, and Verrucomicrobia consistent with higher PTDS symptom ratings. Such bacteria are important for immune control, and their decreased abundance may have led to immune system dysregulation and the development of PTSD symptoms (169). Research using a murine PTSD model (170) has shown that immunization with a heat-killed preparation of the immunoregulatory bacterium Mycobacterium vaccae (NCTC 11659) has caused a more positive behavioral reaction to a psychosocial stressor (171). Studies performed in healthy volunteers have shown that the administration of multiple probiotics has been associated with increased well-being, as well as a decrease in anxiety and psychiatric distress. Both of those results are provisional. There is a growing need for well- designed, double-blind, placebo-controlled clinical trials to assess the effect of bacterial supplementation and controlled dietary improvements on psychiatric effects and cognitive functions of PTSD patients.

The Effects of Meditation and Yoga on PTSD

Scientific data exists for the efficacy of mindfulness-based stress management (MBSR) in PTSD care. Slow respiration and long periods of exhalation during MBSR contribute to an improvement in parasympathetic tone. However, psychiatric trials have proven the efficacy of yoga as a psychological tool for Depression and dissociation by a downregulation of the emotional response. Yoga activities have reduced PSTD symptoms after natural disasters. Anxiety disorders that lead to yoga, including PTSD, go hand in hand with low HRV and low GABA activity. PFC, hippocampus, and

amygdala connections, in combination with feedback from the autonomous nervous system and the GABA system, provide a network by which yoga- based activities can reduce symptoms. There is evidence that incomplete elimination of pathological fear in PTSD is correlated with decreased regulation of the amygdala function by vmPFC. Activation of PFC combined with decreased parasympathetic activity during yoga may enhance the inhibitory function of the amygdala by PFC GABA projections, decrease the over activity of the amygdala, and decrease symptoms of PTSD.

8.4. Vagus nerve related treatment of Trauma

The body experiences other distressing signs of post-traumatic stress— a tightness in the abdomen, a sinking sensation in the stomach, a familiar pain in the mouth, or a constant sense of fatigue. We now understand that as part of the recovery process we have to turn to the body and as a result we have seen an increase in the use of meditation, mindfulness, tai chi, qigong, feldink circle, massage, craniosacral, dietary therapy, and acupuncture for post-traumatic stress disorder.

Such mind-body treatments are helping us to be less passive, less aggressive and less impulsive to stress. We're growing our understanding of the options we need to make us stay grounded and relaxed. We felt in need of this more. One way the mental-body treatments operate is by activating the nerve in the vagus. Awareness of how this nerve works offers a profound understanding of traumatic stress and promotes our healing capacity. The vagus nerve has therefore taken center stage in the treatment of trauma.

"Mind-body treatments work on the nerve of the vagus to help you regain the balance. You may find a number of breath and movement activities in this article, aimed at relaxing and resetting the vagus nerve. By a cycle of self-study and conscious body consciousness, you will continue to develop techniques that help you regain a sense of comfort and recover from trauma. "Effects of Mind-Body Therapy Vagus Nerve Yoga Dr. Arielle Schwartz The utilization of mental-body therapy is correlated with a broad variety of wellness and well-being changes including: physical and mental wellbeing enhancements Reduction. They allow us to focus on our feelings, impulses and behavioral motives. This observational capacity tends to improve tolerance to discomfort which can contribute to reduced emotional reactivity, fear, panic, chronic pain which depression. In fact, mind-body treatments improve self-understanding and the capacity to perceive that person's point of view with understanding.

Moreover, mental-body treatments are successful as they require structural improvements in the autonomic nervous system as determined by improvements in vagus nerve activity. The vagus nerve reaches through the muscles of the nose, inner ear, chest, back, lungs, stomach and intestines from the brainstem down. Mind-body treatments make changes in how we relate ourselves to our surroundings by encouraging a gentle look and allowing us to try new breath or activity patterns that communicate specifically with other parts of the body. Another way that researchers calculate the changes that exist in the vagus nerve is often referred to as respiratory sinus arrhythmia by heart rate variability (HRV). HRV refers to the rhythmic heart rate oscillations that arise with the breath. It's a function of the intervals between beats in the heart. Higher variability in heart rate is associated with a better ability to withstand or rebound from stress, while lower variability in heart rate is correlated with stress and anxiety. You should think of any form of mind-body therapy that improves variation in the heart rate as creating strength and endurance within the autonomic nervous system. As a result, switching between emotions of anticipation and easiness is smoother.

Pain and recuperation of the vagus nerve vagus and pain If we feel a threat (real or perceived) we change the way we breathe. We can get a good picture here by considering the ways animals react to predators. In certain situations, an animal may rapidly breathe into the upper chest which is a protective reaction of the nervous system that allows them to run or fight in a dangerous environment. In other situations, an object may freeze that includes breathing shallowly or holding the air to prevent a predator being detected. This freeze reflex causes the animal to stand very still and is a response to the threat of immobilization. For certain situations, animals are weak and a predator that is not a scavenger can lose interest in a dead animal. Both the freezing and sluggish responses are supported by an evolutionarily older vagus nerve axis as a member of the parasympathetic nervous system.

Most notably, an animal can activate the stress reflex by shaking and breathing in a manner that maintains homeostasis until it's healthy. Nevertheless, we humans will also live for long stretches of time either in high activation (fight and flight) or weak activation (freeze and faint) responses. This appears to be the case where abuse is persistent and prolonged, as in the case of Complex PTSD (more of this can be found here). In fact, we frequently miss the resources to handle difficult or painful experiences. It may result in physical stress and restricted breathing habits that form the foundation of our posture, modes of activity, and general self- sense.

The Vagus Nerve and Trauma Therapy

The Dynamic PTSD Workbook Dr. Arielle Schwartz According to the Polyvagal Theory of Dr. Stephen Porge, a three-part systemic mechanism includes the autonomic nervous system: the dorsal vagal system, the sympathetic nervous system, and the ventral vagal system. The dorsal vagal system is part of the parasympathetic nervous system and is the newest of the systems. In response to life-threatening conditions, the dorsal vagal nerve immobilizes the body by encouraging a shut-down reflex. The sympathetic nervous system, which is comparatively newer to develop, mobilizes the body by triggering the fight-or-flight reflex in response to the threat. Most notably, mental-body interventions help stimulate the ventral vagal system, which is the newest and most advanced of the systems, this mechanism of "social interaction" is the division of the parasympathetic nervous system that lets you calm and communicate with others while you feel healthy.

To help repair the vagus nerve, you will learn practices; but, not all practice is right for everybody. Alternatively, I encourage you to play with and try a range of methods of breathing and action before you discover what fits for you. You will start developing techniques through a cycle of self-study and conscious body consciousness that help you maintain a sense of protection and recover from trauma. Here are few tools to help get you started: Attend your Gut: Dr. Arielle Schwartz Somatic Therapy You can also boost the health of the vagus nerve by ensuring a balanced digestive system. The inner nervous system, also known as the belly brain, is comprised of the "microbiome" that resides in the gut. This habitat includes hundreds of healthy and bacterial organisms that live within the intestinal tracts. An imbalance in your intestine can result in an inflammatory reaction in your immune system and cause a wide range of debilitating symptoms including anxiety and depression. Through rising the sugar intake and finding any latent food intolerances, you will build a balanced microbiota. You may require a doctor or nutritionist's help in finding the causes of a deficiency in the gut; however, the effort it takes to incorporate these improvements into your life is well worth it.

Conclusion

The relationship between the intestine and the brain is based on a dynamic network containing not just neurological but also endocrine, immune, and humoral interactions.

The vagus nerve is an integral part of the brain–good axis and plays a significant role in inflammation regulation, in maintaining intestinal homeostasis, and in controlling food consumption, satiety, and energy homeostasis. It is known that there is a connection between diet and the vagus nerve, and vagal tone can affect food consumption and weight gain.

The vagus nerve also plays a major part in the pathogenesis of mental illnesses, obesity, and other stress-induced and inflammatory diseases. Stimulation of the vagus nerve and multiple mediation methods suggest that manipulation of the vagus nerve has a therapeutic effect, primarily because of its soothing and anti-inflammatory properties.

Extinction, coupled with VNS, is faster than extinction coupled with a sham stimulation. VNS is a widely available and effective alternative to exposure therapy for the treatment of extreme anxiety disorders, as officially approved by the Federal FDA for depression and seizure prevention.

Vagus nerve stimulation is an efficient anticonvulsant tool, which has demonstrated therapeutic efficacy in persistent depression insensitive to therapy in clinical trials. Because in the stress response (LC, orbitofrontal cortex, insula, hippocampus, and amygdala), the vagus nerve sends information to brain regions, this pathway may be involved in the perception or manifestation of various somatic and cognitive symptoms that characterize stress-related disorders.

Psychotropic medications, such as serotonin reuptake inhibitors, have impacts in both the brain and gastrointestinal tract and can thus be known as brain–good axis modulators.

Work exploring the role between dietary factors, somatic factors such as heart rate, psychiatric and pharmacological treatments, and vagal behavior has the ability to contribute to integrative therapeutic strategies that include VNS, medical approaches, drugs, and clinical interventions, such as care-based methods that can be personalized to the individual's needs.

CPSIA information can be obtained
at www.ICGtesting.com
Printed in the USA
BVHW042115240321
603179BV00016B/1192

9 781801 649230